Building Websites with

A Step by Step Tutorial

Hagen Graf

BIRMINGHAM - MUMBAI

Building Websites with Mambo
A Step by Step Tutorial

First published: August 2005.

Published by Packt Publishing Ltd.
32 Lincoln Road
Olton
Birmingham, B27 6PA, UK.

ISBN 1-904811-73-6

www.packtpub.com

Cover Design by www.visionwt.com

First published in the German language as:

"Mambo Websites organisieren und gestalten mit dem Open Source-CMS" by Addison-Wesley, an imprint of Pearson Education Deutschland GmbH.

Credits

Author
Hagen Graf

Translator
Wolfgang Spegg

Technical Editors
Abhishek Shirodkar
Paramita Chakrabarti

Cover Designer
Helen Wood

Proofreaders
Chris Smith
Richard Deeson

Layout
Abhishek Shirodkar
Paramita Chakrabarti

Illustrators
Dinesh Kandalgaonkar
Nilesh Mohite
Manjiri Nadkarni

About the Author

Hagen Graf was born in July 1964. Born and raised in Lower Saxony, Germany, his first contact with a computer was in the late seventies with a Radioshack TRS 80.

As a salesperson, he organized his customers' data by programming suitable applications. This gave him a big advantage over other salesmen. With the intention of honing his skills, he joined evening courses in programming and became a programmer.

Nowadays he works in his wife's consulting company as a trainer, consultant, and programmer (`http://alternative-unternehmensberatung.de`).

Hagen Graf has published two other books in German, about the Apache web server and about security problems in Windows XP. Since 2001, he has been engaged in a nonprofit e-learning community called "machm-it.org e.V.", as well as in several national and international projects. All the projects are related to content management, community building, and harnessing the power of social software like wikis and weblogs.

He chose Mambo CMS because of its simplicity and easy-to-use administration. You can access and comment on his blog (`http://hagen.take-part.org`).

For the first time in my life, one of my books has been translated from German to English. I wish to thank the team of Packt Publishing, especially Louay, Wolfgang, Michelle, Abhishek, and Paramita for making this possible. I also wish to thank the Miro and Mambo team, especially Alex Kempkens and Brian Teeman. They have done a very good job.

Acknowledgement

This book was developed during the course of a trip. First, I would like to thank the many café owners who allowed me to plug my computer into a socket free of charge. I would also like to encourage the hotspot operators to create more WLAN places in the world and not to make access too expensive. A commendable example of this is the very friendly Wifirst in Paris (`http://www.wifirst.fr/index.jsp`), which together with the Metro operator RATP (`http://www.ratp.fr/`) operates an affordable WLAN at many Paris locations.

In addition, I wish to thank my daughter Isabell (`http://www.isapisa.de/`) and my wife Christine for their help and encouragement. I also wish to praise Skype (`http://www.skype.com/`) and Jabber (`http://www.jabber.org`) project; without these two, our communication with editorial team would not have been possible.

Alex Kempkens (`http://www.thinknetwork.com/`), development team member of Mambo, author of the Mambelfish component and the editor for the German book project deserve special thanks for their patience in reading the manuscript and the suggestions they made. And without Boris Karnikowski's (editor of the book at Addison Wesley) integral strengths, you surely would not be holding this book in your hands.

Most of all, I want to thank you, my readers. Let me know how you liked the book!

Hagen Graf (`hagen@sit2000.de`)

August 2005.

Table of Contents

Introduction

Mambo is a piece of software that makes it easy to administer content. I will describe this administration of content in detail during the course of this book. This book about Mambo is being developed on a trip: I am constantly on the move while attending to my work. My work consists of activities such as lecturing, advising, listening, testing and trying, programming, learning how to understand structures, trying to get to the bottom of things, and constantly testing. So, why am I writing a book about content management while I am on the road?

Well, the world has become more mobile in the last few years. "More mobile" means that even the laptops bought at the supermarket will operate on battery for more than four hours. Their screens are readable in sunlight. Wireless Internet hotspots are affordable.

But more mobility also means customers from different countries, with different languages and cultures can now interact without ever meeting. This means long road, rail, or air trips for the necessary, but less frequent personal meetings and short response times for customers' e-mail inquiries. The charming 24/7 abbreviation hits mobility's nail on the head—24 hours a day, 7 days a week.

Mobility has ramifications on what we used to call an office as well. Five years ago, it was normal to store e-mails on your home or office computer. Today, various service providers are offering almost inexhaustible disk space for these purposes.

In larger companies, terminal servers are becoming more and more influential. The bandwidth of Internet connections is increasing. All this means that you are no longer tied to your home PC, but can access your pool of e-mails, pictures, and documents from any Internet café. This makes you more independent, since your office is suddenly located at any place with a browser and an Internet connection.

In the eighties, Sun Microcomputers proclaimed, "The net is the computer". With the increasing proliferation of web-based applications such as e-mail services, online banking, group calendars, document-management systems, communities, dating services, and online auctions, this claim has become a reality today. Your own terminal is increasingly becoming less important. Even mobile telephones today can send and receive e-mails, take and send photographs, and do much more.

Today, a company, an institution, an association, or an organization needs an Internet presence that is also mobile—one that is in tune with the times, can be easily modified from a browser, and can also be expanded without complication. This website is the place where you will explain to others what you do and what your company does.

It is the place that is available 24 hours a day, 7 days a week to enable you to maintain your customer relations. Until recently, the production of such a homepage was a difficult task. You didn't have to be a designated specialist, but needed perseverance and interest to make the result more appealing. You had to create static HTML pages with an HTML editor and subsequently load them onto the server via File Transfer Protocol. To provide even the simplest interactivity, like a guest book or a forum, you had to learn a programming language. Many people, for understandable reasons, were reluctant to take on this hardship and handed over the production of their homepage either to a web agency or decided not to start such a project at all.

However, rescue is near, because now there is Mambo!

This book deals with the production of a simple website. We use the Mambo Content Management System to do that and show how an attractive, interactive homepage can be created and maintained without programming knowledge and without recourse to an HTML editor.

This website resides on a central server. Access to all functions is available from any terminal with an Internet connection. This means that you can maintain and update your website from any Internet café in the world or even from your mobile telephone.

Enjoy the experience of learning in the world of Mambo!

What This Book Covers

Mambo is a full-featured content management system that can be used for everything—from simple websites to complex corporate applications. This book begins by introducing the basic principles that underlie the operation of Mambo.

Chapter 1 explains the difficulty of defining a term such as 'content management'. It explores the structure of a CMS and lists the various features of Mambo. To get an overview of the areas of application for Mambo, a few Mambo-based websites are used as examples.

Chapter 2 guides us through the process of installing Mambo in an appropriate server environment. It lists the prerequisites for Windows and Linux, and cites the need for selecting a directory for installation.

Chapter 3 guides us through a tour of the created homepage and *Chapter 4* deals with the customization of Mambo, according to the users' needs. It shows us how to install a local language file for different users. It also explains the configuration of Mambo administration and shows us how to install new Mambots.

Chapter 5 deals with the creation of extensions. Few content management systems provide web accessibility for users with disabilities and Mambo is one of them. The xMambo project tries to make Mambo web pages usable by people with disabilities.

Chapter 6 explains the corporate identity of an enterprise. It studies the Internet technologies that Mambo works with— HTML/XHTML, CSS, and XML. It also shows us how to create our own template packages. *Chapter 7* teaches us how to extend the functional range of Mambo with new components, modules, and Mambots.

Appendix A provides a list of necessary software packages. It also guides us about what to do if we forget our admin password.

What You Need for Using This Book

The prerequisite for this book is a working installation of Mambo. To run Mambo, the typical environment consists of PHP/Apache/MySQL. We cover the details of installation in Chapter 2.

Conventions

In this book, you will find a number of styles of text that distinguish between different kinds of information. Here are some examples of these styles, and an explanation of their meaning.

There are three styles for code. Code words in text are shown as follows:

Create a subdirectory called com_mambobook under the [mambo]/administration /components/ directory.

A block of code will appear as follows:

```
// Examine access rights
if (!($acl->acl_check( 'administration', 'edit', 'users',
$my->usertype, 'components', 'all' ) | $acl->acl_check(
'administration', 'edit', 'users', $my->usertype, 'components',
'com_newsfeeds' ))) {
mosRedirect( 'index2.php', _NOT_AUTH );
```

When we wish to draw your attention to a particular part of a code block, the relevant lines or items will be made bold:

```
'com_newsfeeds' ))) {
mosRedirect( 'index2.php', _NOT_AUTH );
```

New terms and **important words** are introduced in a bold-type font. Words that you see on the screen, in menus or dialog boxes for example, appear in our text like this: "clicking the Next button moves you to the next screen".

Tips, suggestions, or important notes appear in a box like this.

Reader Feedback

Feedback from our readers is always welcome. Let us know what you think about this book, what you liked or may have disliked. Reader feedback is important for us to develop titles that you really get the most out of. To send us general feedback, simply drop an e-mail to feedback@packtpub.com, making sure to mention the book title in the subject of your message.

If there is a book that you need and would like to see us publish, please send us a note in the SUGGEST A TITLE form on www.packtpub.com or e-mail title@packtpub.com. If there is a topic that you have expertise in and you are interested in either writing or contributing to a book, see our author guide on www.packtpub.com/authors.

Customer Support

Now that you are the proud owner of a Packt book, we have a number of things to help you to get the most from your purchase.

Code Download

Visit http://www.packtpub.com/support, and select this book from the list of titles to download any example code or extra resources for this book. The files available for download will then be displayed.

> The downloadable files contain instructions on how to use them.

Errata

Although we have taken every care to ensure the accuracy of our content, mistakes do happen. If you find a mistake in one of our books—maybe a mistake in text or code—we would be grateful if you would report it to us. By doing this you can save other readers from frustration, and help to improve subsequent versions of this book. If you find any errata, report them by visiting http://www.packtpub.com/support, selecting your book, clicking on the Submit Errata link, and entering the details of your errata. Once your errata have been verified, your submission will be accepted and the errata added to the list of existing errata. The existing errata can be viewed by selecting your title from http://www.packtpub.com/support.

Questions

You can contact us at questions@packtpub.com if you are having a problem with some aspect of the book, and we will do our best to address it.

1

Terms and Concepts

Before you can understand how to operate Mambo, you need to understand the basic principles that underlie the system.

1.1 Content Management System

Content Management System (CMS) contains the terms **content** and **management** (administration) that imprecisely refer to a system that administers content. Such a system could be a board and a piece of chalk (menu or school chalkboard), or it could be something like Wikipedia (the free online encyclopedia at http://www.wikipedia.org), or an online auction house such as eBay (http://www.ebay.com/). In these cases contents and participants are administered. These participants play a major role with CMS, on one hand as administrators and on the other hand as users.

But it gets even better. Apart from CMSs there are **Enterprise Resource Planning Systems (ERP**, administration of corporate data), **Customer Relationship Management Systems (CRM**, care of customer contacts), **Document Management Systems (DMS**, administration of documents), **Human Resource Management Systems (HRM**, administration of staffing), and many others.

An operating system such as Windows or Linux also administers content. It is difficult to define the term CMS because of its encompassing nature and variety of functions.

Lately **ECMS** has established itself as the nickname for **Enterprise Content Management Systems**. The other abbreviations listed above are the subsets of ECMS. Mambo belongs to the category of **Web Content Management Systems (WCMS)**, since it exclusively administers content on a web server.

Since these terms are still relatively new in the enterprise world, these systems will surely be developed even further. In principle, however, there will always be an integration system that tries to interconnect all these systems. In general, the term 'content management' is used in connection with web pages that can be maintained by a browser. This doesn't necessarily make the definition any easier.

1.2 A Quick Glance into History

While the Sun maintained in the nineties that "the Network is the computer", Microsoft was not going to rest until a Windows computer sat on every desk.

The computer that Microsoft was concerned with was a mixture of data files and binary executable files. Files with executable binary contents are called **programs**, and were bought and installed by customers to manipulate data. Microsoft Office was the winner in most of the offices around the world. The computer that Sun was working with was a cheap, dumb terminal with a screen, a keyboard, a mouse, and access to the Internet. The programs and data were not stored on this computer, but somewhere on the net.

The *mine* philosophy governed Microsoft's practices whereas the *our* philosophy was adopted by Sun. The motivation for these philosophies was not for pure humanitarian reasons, but for economic interest. Primarily, Microsoft sold software for PCs to the consumer market, Sun, on the other hand, sold server hardware and programs to the enterprise market.

The Internet, invented in the sixties, spread like an explosion in the mid-nineties. Among other things, **Hyper Text Markup Language (HTML)**, the language used to write web pages, and the development of web servers and web clients (browsers) helped its expansion. The Internet itself was a set of rules that could be understood by different devices and was developed so skillfully that it covered the entire planet in almost no time.

An individual without an e-mail address could no longer be reached and a company without a website was not only old-fashioned, but didn't exist in the eyes of many customers. The whole world swarmed to the Internet within a short time to become a part of it. Movies like *The Matrix* (http://whatisthematrix.warnerbros.com/) became huge hits and *1984* (http://en.wikipedia.org/wiki/1984), a book by George Orwell, was forgotten.

New net citizens on one hand came from the *mine* world and on the other hand from the *our* world. Those who were used to buying programs bought HTML editors and created Internet pages with them. The others preferred to write their own HTML code with any text editor they had on hand. And the web agency, where one could order a homepage, was born.

Both groups faced the problem that HTML pages were static. To change the contents of the page, it had to be modified on a PC and then copied to the server. This was not only awkward and expensive, but also made web presences like eBay or Amazon (http://amazon.com/) impossible. Both groups found more or less good solutions for this problem.

The *mine* faction, developed fast binary programs, with which one could produce HTML pages, and load them via automated procedures onto the server. Interactive elements, such as visitor counters, among others, were built into such pages.

The *our* faction discovered Java applets and with them the capability of writing a program that resided centrally on a server, which was operated via a browser. Entire business ideas were based on this solution—like online booking and flight reservation concepts. Both groups tried to develop market share in different ways.

The result was quite a stable market for both, in which passionate battles over the correct operating system (Windows, Linux, or Mac OS X) constantly drove the version numbers higher and higher. Customers got used to the fact that the whole thing wasn't that easy.

There is always a third option in these situations. As in our case, it was the emergence of open-source scripting languages like PHP (http://www.php.net/). Rasmus Lerdorf had the goal of offering interactive elements on his homepage and with that a new programming language was born. From the outset, PHP was optimized in a perfect cooperation with the MySQL database, which also worked on the GNU/GPL platform (http://www.gnu.org/licenses/gpl.html).

Fortunately, on the server there was a Linux operating system and an Apache web server that offered the necessary infrastructure. Display medium at the client side was the browser, which was certainly available. Soon **LAMP** (Linux, Apache, MySQL, and PHP) became synonymous with database-supported, interactive presence on the Internet.

The most diverse systems like forums, communities, online shops, voting pages, and similar things that made it possible to organize contents with the help of a browser were developed in an enthusiastic creative rush.

After 'difficult' things such as Linux and Apache, 'soft' products were developed. The nineties were nearing their end; the Internet share bubble burst and suddenly the trend was to build unmitigated classical business models with unmitigated classical methods.

Whenever the economy isn't doing well, costs are scrutinized and the possibility of lowering costs is contemplated. There are now, as there were earlier, numerous possibilities. PHP applications always had distribution numbers in the millions. Only the **phpBB** (http://www.phpbb.com/) and **phpMyAdmin** (http://www.phpmyadmin.net) projects are mentioned here as examples. One was developed into the quasi-standard for forum software, the other one into the standard for manipulating MySQL databases via web interfaces. The source code of the PHP language and that of applications were improved because they had an enormous number of users and developers.

The more open a project was, the more successful it became. Individual gurus were able to save enterprises immense costs in the shortest time. Static HTML pages were considered old and expensive and were overhauled. They had to be dynamic! Developers have been working in this environment for a few years now. Linux, Apache, MySQL, and PHP are readily accepted in industry. The search for professionally usable PHP applications has begun.

With this search one looks for:

- A simple installation process
- Easy serviceability of the source code
- Security of the source code
- User-friendliness
- Easy expandability

The special advantage of PHP applications is the independence from hardware and operating system. LAMP also exists as WAMP (Windows, Apache, MySQL, and PHP) for Windows, MAMP (Mac, Apache, MySQL, and PHP) for Apple, and for numerous other platforms. And now finally our Mambo comes into the fray.

1.2.1 Mambo

The Australian company Miro (http://www.miro.com.au/) developed a CMS with the name of **Mambo** in the year 2001. It made this system available as open-source software, to test it and to make sure of a wider distribution. In the year 2002, the company split its product Mambo into a commercial and an open-source version. The commercial variant was called **Mambo CMS**, the open-source version **Mambo Open Source** (MOS). In the meantime all parties involved have agreed that MOS can officially be called Mambo and together a successful future for the fastest developing CMS of the moment is secured (http://www.mamboserver.com/index.php?option=com_content&task=view&id= 14&Itemid=0).

The advantages of the commercial version for companies are primarily in increased security and that they have the company Miro as a partner that also supports further development. The advantage the open-source version offers is that it is free and an enormous community of users and developers alike provide continuous enhancements. In addition, it is possible for enterprises to take Mambo as a base and to build their own solutions on top of it.

1.3 Structure of a CMS

1.3.1 Frontend and Backend

A CMS consists of a frontend and a backend. The frontend is the website—what the visitors and the logged-on users see.

The backend, on the other hand, contains the administration layer of the website for the administrator. Configuration, maintenance, cleaning, creation of statistics, and new content creation are all done in the backend. The backend is at a different **Uniform Resource Locator (URL)** than the website.

1.3.2 Access Rights

Whenever we talk of management, we talk of the clever administration of existing resources. In a CMS, usernames are assigned to people involved and these are provided with different access rights. This ranges from a simple registered user through an 'author' and 'editor' up to the 'super-administrator', who has full control over the domain. Based on the rights, the website then displays different content, or the user works in administrative areas apart from the website.

1.3.3 Content

We handle all kinds of content; in the simplest case, it is text. But content can also be a picture, a link, a piece of music, or a combination of everything. To keep an overview of the content, one embeds it in structures, for example, texts of different categories. The categories, of course, are also content that need to be administered.

1.3.4 Templates

A template is a kind of visual edit format that is placed on top of content. A template defines the colors, character fonts, character sizes, background pictures, spacing, and partitioning of the page—in other words, everything that has to do with the appearance of the page.

1.3.5 Extensions (Components)

Every system has to be expandable and be able to grow with the requirements. Functionalities that belong into one context are also covered by the term **components**. For example, typical components are an online shop, a user manager, a newsletter maintenance system, or a forum. Components contain the business logic of their page.

Modules within the components are used to integrate content in the desired form into templates. For example, a recent news module supplies the headings of the five most recent pieces of news to the template. Another module delivers the number of users that are online at the time, or the meteorological data for your current town or city.

1.3.6 Workflow

By workflow one understands a work routine. The bureaucratic set of three (mark, punch, and file) is an example of a workflow. A recipe for baking a cake is a workflow. Since several people usually work with CMS content, well-organized workflows are a genuine help. In this connection, one sometimes speaks of work supplies that a certain user has.

For example, the editor sees a list of posted pieces of news, which he or she has to examine for correctness. After examining, the editor marks the pieces of news as correct and they appear in the work supply of the publisher. The publisher then decides whether to publish the piece on the front page.

1.3.7 Configuration Settings

Settings that apply to the entire website are specified using the configuration settings. This includes the title text in the browser window, passwords for search engines, switches that permit or forbid logging on to the site, or that switch the entire page offline or online, and many other functions.

1.4 Mambo as Real Estate

Mambo is a kind of construction kit that lets you, once it is installed on the server, create and maintain your website. Mambo is like a house that you build on a property of your choice and that you can furnish gradually. Thus, to a certain extent, it is real estate.

Stop! I was talking about mobility all the time and now I'm asking you to build real estate? Have no fear, the real estate you build, is physically at one place (your server), but is accessible from every place. To make a piece of real estate habitable, you need necessary services such as heating, electricity, and water supply. That is the reason your Mambo is deposited at as safe a server as possible, where hopefully the electricity will never be cut. Think of the abbreviation 24/7.

Just like your house, you also have a certain room layout in Mambo. You have a room for presentations, for cooking and talking, for working, and a completely private one that you only show to good friends. Perhaps you also have a large room that integrates all areas.

It doesn't matter which room layout you decide on. You have to furnish your house, lay a beautiful floor, paper the walls, hang a few pictures, and of course, clean it regularly. The numerous guests leave traces that are not always desirable. To find your house the visitors need an address. This address has to be familiar to as many people as possible. Since there is no residents' registration office on the Internet, you have to be the one that takes care of the topic, "How can I be found?"

Perhaps you also have a garden that surrounds your house and has different entry gates. There is an official entrance portal, a back door, and perhaps another small, weathered garden gate for good friends.

And perhaps you don't like such houses and would rather use trailers, tents, mobile homes, hotels, or maybe prefer community living and are glad to pay rent and don't want to think about all the details.

If you apply the last few sentences to your website, then you are already noticing how important it is to know what you want, who you are, and how you want to look at your community. One cannot *not* communicate! One can, however, be quickly misunderstood.

So plan your website on the Internet properly. Put thought into the texts, into possible interactive elements like a calendar or a forum, and of course, an area that only registered users are allowed to see.

Think about what prompts that move and don't patronize users. Take a look at how others do it. Talk with the people you want to address through your website and invest your heart and soul into those things that are absolutely crucial for the success of your entry.

1.4.1 Mambo Versions

As with all software, there are different development versions with Mambo. This book is concerned with version 4.5.2. As you can see from the relatively high version number, Mambo is quite developed and tested.

Versions 4.5.1, 4.5.2, 4.5.3, and 4.5.4 released in 2005 are compatible with one another. This compatibility is important with security updates and with the use of external components and modules. A guest book component that was written for version 4.5.1 also runs under version 4.5.2 and subsequent versions.

A previously planned version 4.6 is not going to be released. The current road map was published at the end of February 2005 (`http://mamboserver.com/menu/ Mambo_4.5_and_5.0_Roadmap/`). The next version jump will be released in the beginning of the year 2006 with version Mambo 5. At this time, the version carousel is still turning quite rapidly with Mambo. Version 5.0, however, will bring with it a slowdown in development.

Regardless of which version you use, the fundamental concepts and application flow are the same in all versions.

1.4.2 Mambo Features

Mambo is a full-featured content management system that can be used for everything— from simple websites to complex corporate applications. Here is a listing of Mambo features in bullet form:

- Free source code
- Large and eager community of users and developers
- Simple workflow system

- Caching mechanism to secure fast page creation with favorite pages
- Waste paper basket
- Banner management
- Data manager for uploading and administering data
- Publication system for content
- Content summaries in RSS format
- Search-engine-friendly URLs
- Multilingual frontend
- Macro language for data content (Mambots)
- Administration interface that is separated from the homepage
- Simple, expandable template, and component system
- Simple, but powerful template system (HTML, CSS, PHP) without a complicated template language
- Hierarchical user groups
- Simple visitor statistics
- WYSIWYG editor for content
- Simple polling
- System of evaluation for contents
- Many free extensions at `http://www.mamboforge.net`, for instance, forums
- Picture galleries
- Document Management Systems (DMS)
- Templates
- Calendar
- And much more

1.4.3 Examples of Mambo Pages

Now we take a look at a few Mambo-based websites. To get an overview of the areas of application for Mambo, here is a selection independent of content:

Water and Stone, Thailand: A web and print media design company:

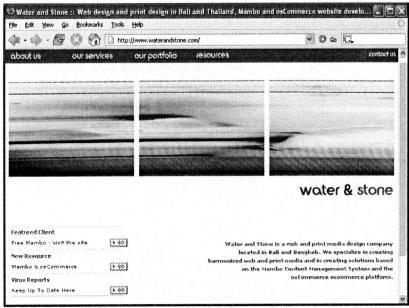

Figure 1.1: Water and Stone, Thailand

Flam Player, Canada: A Macromedia Flash-based MP3 player:

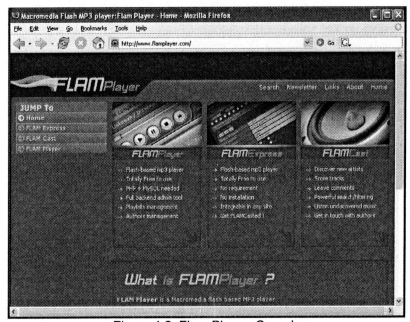

Figure 1.2: Flam Player, Canada

Airline Pilot Central, Canada: A company providing pay and benefit information for airline pilots, fleet breakdowns and pilot hiring status for US and Canadian airlines:

Figure 1.3: Airline Pilot Central, Canada

Elektronics, Poland: A wholesaler of lighting and electric installation accessories:

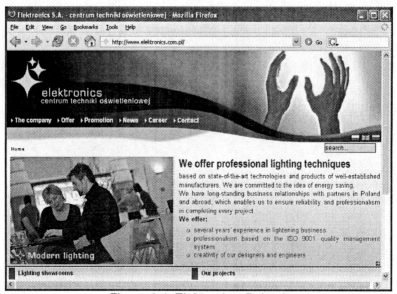

Figure 1.4: Elektronics, Poland

Further examples of Mambo pages can be found at:

`http://www.mamboawards.com/`

and in the gallery at:

`http://www.mamboserver.com/`

Have fun poking around, it's worth it!

2
Installation

In this chapter, we will go through the process of installing and running Mambo. To install Mambo, we must have the dream team mentioned in Chapter 1 installed as the development environment: Apache, MySQL, and PHP.

Mambo does not make any special demands on Apache or MySQL. PHP has to be of version 4.1.2 or higher and it should be compiled with support for MySQL and Zlib. Zlib is a library that makes it possible for PHP to read file packages that are compressed with the ZIP procedure.

We can use any web server that works with PHP (`http://en.wikipedia.org/wiki/web_server`). From version 4.5.3 of Mambo, it will be possible to use databases other than MySQL. The installation has to be done on a server that can be accessed over the Internet, usually located at the Internet provider.

Before we venture into the wilderness of the Internet, we should first practice on our local computer. This is an advantage as there are no connection fees, it is very fast, and we can practice at a leisurely pace. We can even have a small local network at home where we can install Mambo on one computer and access it from another.

All the necessary downloads discussed in this book can be downloaded from `http://www.alternative-unternehmensberatung.de/component/option,com _weblinks/catid,2/Itemid,40/lang,en/`. A list of file packages can be found in the Appendix. These files are suitable for local installation, since the examples in this book can be reconstructed that way.

Remember, however, there are more current versions on the respective project sites on the Internet. If you install Mambo *in the wild*, on a server on the Internet, you should always use the latest stable version.

2.1 Setting Up the Local Server Environment

To install Mambo locally, we have to set up the appropriate server environment.

2.1.1 Windows

Due to the user-friendliness of Windows, over 90 percent of computers work with Windows as operating system. Unfortunately, Apache web server, MySQL database, and PHP are not included with Windows. A practical approach would be to install each of these programs separately, or grab a preconfigured package.

Log on to the system in administrator mode. To check your account type, click Start | Control Panel | User Accounts and change it to Computer administrator if required:

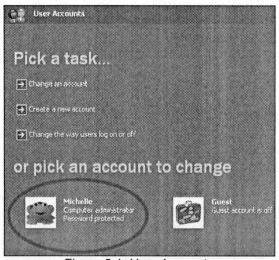

Figure 2.1: User Accounts

XAMPP for Windows

XAMPP is a project of Kai 'Oswald' Seidler and Kay Vogelgesang. These two have been creating a complete development environment with the ingredients Apache, MySQL, PHP, Perl, and various extensions for several years.

XAMPP can be downloaded from http://www.apachefriends.org/en/xampp.html as zip archives for various operating systems. This is an immense advantage for people like you and me, who are primarily interested in Mambo and not so much in how all of it works. Also, the entire installation can be removed from the computer with one mouse-click without leaving a trace. To download and install XAMPP:

1. Download the xampplite-win32-1.4.14.zip file from http://www.apachefriends.org/en/xampp-windows.html#641 and extract it on the local drive:

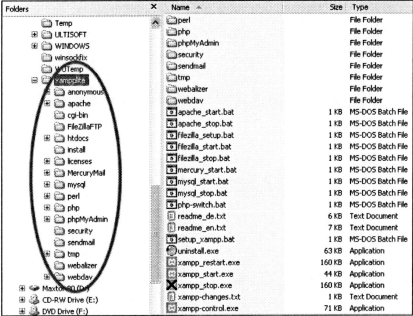

Figure 2.2: Xampplite Directory

2. Open the setup_xampp.bat file from the xampplite folder. XAMPP makes no entries in the Windows Registry and sets no system variables:

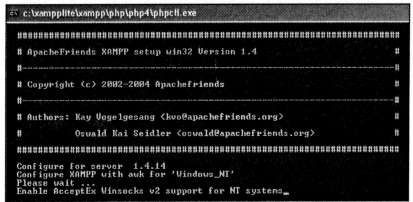

Figure 2.3: Execute Setup_xampp.bat

3. PHP starts automatically as a module. To start Apache, open the apache_start.bat file from the xampplite folder. A command request window opens, which indicates that Apache has started:

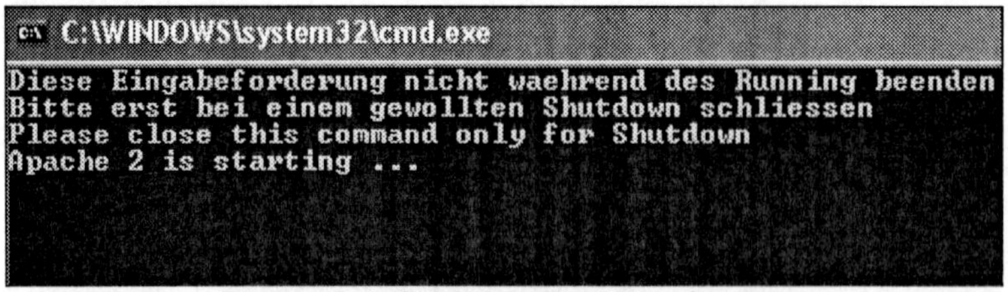

Figure 2.4: Start Apache Web Server

The command request can be minimized, but closing it will terminate Apache web server.

4. Start MySQL by opening the mysql_start.bat file. As opposed to Apache, MySQL has a separate script to terminate itself. To accomplish this, open the mysql_stop.bat file.

Figure 2.5: Start MySQL

5. Open the website http://127.0.0.1/ or http://localhost/ to check if XAMPP is correctly installed. On the XAMPP start page, click on the English link and the start page shows up (Figure 2.6).

The document directory of your website is htdocs in the xampplite folder. This directory contains all the pages that are accessible by a remote computer on the Internet.

More information on usernames and passwords can be found in the readme_en.txt file. To uninstall the package, close all current servers and delete the xampplite directory.

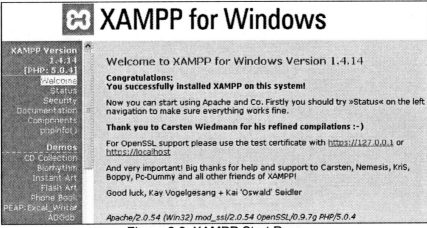
Figure 2.6: XAMPP Start Page

Mambo Stand Alone Server

The **Mambo Stand Alone Server (MSAS)** project offers complete installation of Mambo 4.5.2, Apache, PHP, MySQL, and phpMyAdmin. The setup `msas452-setup.exe` file can be downloaded from `http://www.mambosolutions.com/main/content/view/13/59/`. After the installation, we get an executable Mambo system in the `MSAS` folder. Since this book covers the installation of Mambo, xampplite has been used.

2.1.2 Linux

With Linux everything is usually simple. Different distributions with different standard configurations are available. Usually our dream team is pre-installed and just needs to be started. An XAMPP version can also be installed for Linux. My opinion, however, is that it makes more sense to grab the original programs. The installation is done by a package manager and is very simple.

SUSE (9.1)

With the help of a configuration program YaST, you can check whether Apache, MySQL, and PHP are already installed. If that is not the case, select the appropriate packages for installation and let YaST install them. These are the packages in detail:

- `apache2`, `apache2-level`, and `apache2-mod_php4`
- `mysql` and `php4-mysql`

You can find these packages via the YaST interface on your SUSE distribution media or on the Internet:

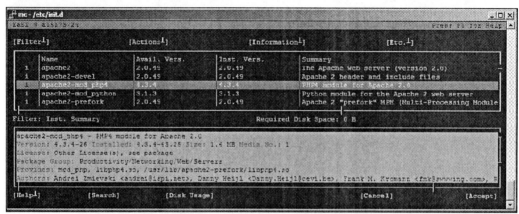

Figure 2.7: YaST Accessed from a Windows PC in a Shell

Start the Apache web server with the command /etc/init.d/apache2ctl start and the MySQL database server with /etc/init.d/mysql start.

You can stop both the servers with the command stop. By typing help, you get an overview of all parameters.

Debian 3.1/Sarge

With Debian, the agent of choice is apt. You can install Apache, MySQL, and PHP with the program apt.

apt-get install [packetname]

The following are the packages in detail:

- apache-common: Support files for all Apache web servers
- php4: A server-side, HTML-embedded scripting language
- mysql-common: MySQL database common files (e.g. /etc/mysql/my.cnf)
- mysql-server: MySQL database server binaries

You can find these packages automatically over the Internet or on the Debian CD/DVD by using apt.

Then start Apache with the command /etc/init.d/apachectl start and MySQL with /etc/init.d/mysql start.

Your Own Server at a Provider

If you have rented a complete server from a provider, then you usually have a shell entrance and free choice of the Linux distribution that you want to use. In addition, the system is preconfigured and contains all necessary file packages and configurations. Usually special administration interfaces, such as, Confixx (`http://www.sw-soft.com/en/products/confixx/`) or Visas are used for configuring these servers. You can comfortably start, stop, and configure your server and the Apache and MySQL services from a browser interface with this tool.

2.2 On a Virtual Server in the Net

The hosting industry changes very rapidly. Check out the forum on `http://mamboserver.com/` for actual hints about installing Mambo on different servers.

2.3 Installing Mambo

To install Mambo, download the latest stable version `MamboV4.5.2-stable.tar.gz` from `http://mamboforge.net/frs/?group_id=5`.

2.3.1 Selecting a Directory for Installation

One has to decide whether Mambo needs to be installed directly into a document directory or a subdirectory. This is important, since many users prefer a short URL to their homepage.

An Example

If Mambo is unzipped directly in `/htdocs`, the web page starts when the domain name `http://www.myhomepage.com` is accessed from its local computer `http://localhost/` and/or from the server on the Internet. If subdirectories are created under `/htdocs/`, for example, `/htdocs/mymambo/` and we unzip the package there, we have to enter `http://localhost/mymambo/` in the browser. This isn't a problem locally, but doesn't look good on a production Internet page.

Some HTML files and subdirectories, however, are already in `/htdocs` in the local xampplite environment under Windows, which, for example, displays the greetings page of xampplite (as shown in Figure 2.6). In a local Linux environment, a starting page dependent on the distribution and the web server settings is also displayed.

2.3.2 Local Installation of Mambo

Directory

In Windows, create a subdirectory named mambo under the document directory by using Windows Explorer. The directory tree in Windows Explorer should look like this:

Figure 2.8: Mambo Directory

In Linux, use the shell KDE Konqueror or Midnight Commander:

[Document home]/htdocs/mambo/

An empty index appears in the xampplite version when the URL http://localhost/mambo is entered in the browser:

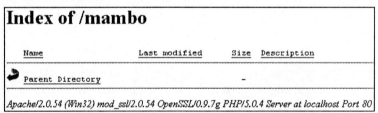

Figure 2.9: Apache Directory Display

With Linux or with another configuration it can happen that you don't get a message and therefore you don't have access to this directory. This depends on the configuration of the web server. For security reasons, the automatic directory display is often deactivated. A potential hacker could draw many interesting conclusions about the directory structure and the files on your homepage. From this information the hacker could target your computer for hacking.

Unpacking

In Windows XP the MamboV4.5.2-stable.tar.gz file can be directly unpacked from Windows Explorer. In all other versions of Windows a separate unpacking program is

required, for example, the shareware program Filzip that can be downloaded from
http://www.filzip.com/en/index.html.
In Linux, type the following command to unpack the file package, called a **compressed
tarball**, in the prepared directory:

```
-zxvf MamboV4.5.2-stable.tar.gz
```

After unpacking, the following directories and files can be seen in Windows Explorer:

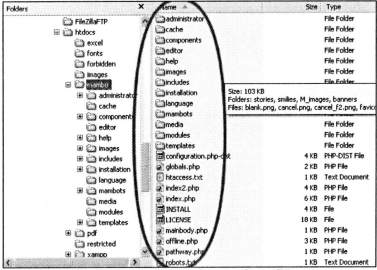

Figure 2.10: Mambo Source Code Files

This structure is same on all operating systems—only the presentation differs. The
following figure shows a presentation in an FTP client where the local PC is in the left
window and the remote web server in the right:

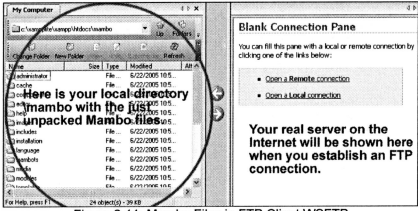

Figure 2.11: Mambo Files in FTP Client WSFTP

Mambo Web Installer

From now on, everything is going to go lightning fast because the Mambo web installer will be taking over command. Go to the URL `http://localhost/mambo/` where the web installer announces itself with a pre-installation check. This check determines whether your environment is suitable for installing Mambo. If there are many green test results, then it is already a good sign. Depending on your configuration there can be differences here.

The web installer takes the configuration settings of Apache, PHP, and the operating system into consideration. On Linux-based systems, attention should be given to writing rights. If you are working with the xampplite solution under Windows, the web installer should look as shown in the following figure:

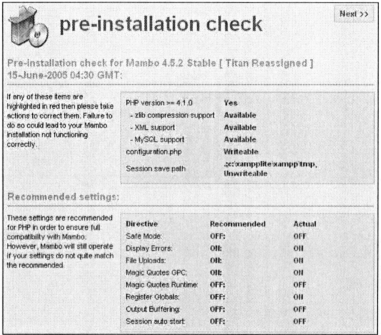

Figure 2.12: Pre-Installation Check

Click on Next to get the announcement of the GNU/GPL license, which you must accept by marking the I Accept the GPL License field. The installation with the web installer takes place in the following four steps:

Step 1

Database parameters are queried in a questionnaire. You can set up as many databases as required in xampplite server environment. As there is a MySQL user set up with the name root without a password, enter the name of a database that doesn't exist yet in the installer. Users usually have the rights to access databases in a working environment. Enter the following parameters in a local xampplite installation:

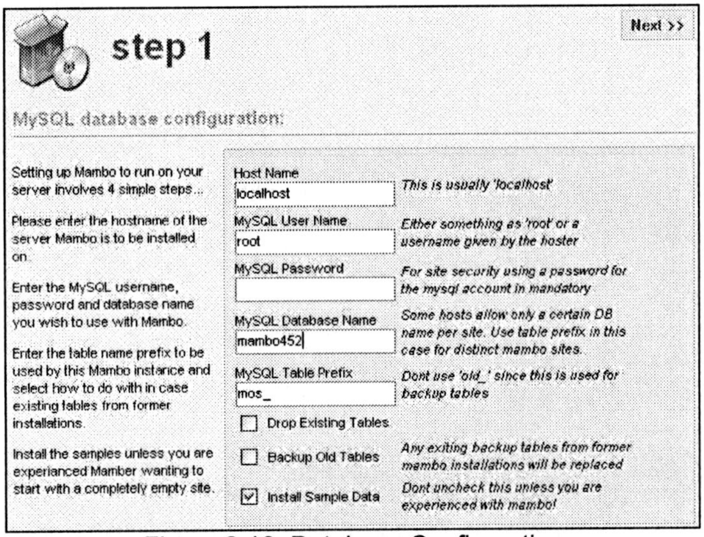

Figure 2.13: Database Configuration

Host Name: localhost

MySQL User Name: root

MySQL Password: (leave this empty—but be aware of the security risk!)

MySQL Database Name: mambo452

MySQL Table Prefix: The web installer writes the text that is entered in the field before producing each table. By default, the web installer suggests mos _, because sometimes you get only one MySQL database from an Internet provider.

If two Mambo pages are required to be operated, there would be a problem, since you cannot differentiate one table from the other. By means of Table Name Prefix, it is possible to keep apart the tables of different Mambo installations (mambosmith_ or mambojones_). At this time you should accept the default mos_.

Drop Existing Tables: If you are dealing with a 'new' installation into an empty database, do not check this check box. If there is an old version of Mambo in your database, you can overwrite the old files by checking this check box.

Backup Old Tables: With Mambo, data security (backups) can be set up. The backups are stored in special backup tables. To replace old backup tables, check this check box.

Install Sample Data: By default, this check box is checked. This fills your homepage with sample data so that you get a conception of its appearance down the road. Fill your installation with these sample data; we will work with them later on in the book.

Click on the Next button. After a security question, asking whether the installation should indeed go ahead, the web installer creates the database and the appropriate tables.

Step 2

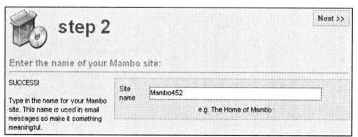

Figure 2.14: Site Name

In step 2, you secure the name of your website. This name shows up in the header of the browser window when someone accesses your website. This name is also used in other places, for example, with confirmation e-mails to registered users. Select a meaningful name. For our example page, we have chosen the name mambo452. Click on Next to set the name.

Step 3

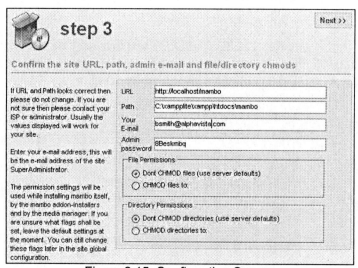

Figure 2.15: Confirmation Screen

In step 3 you must confirm a few basic settings. These settings are important as they permit the Mambo system navigation on your server.

URL: This is the URL of your homepage.

Path: This is the file path on your server that leads to your homepage. In our case it is in the Windows environment.

Your E-Mail: Enter your e-mail address. As a Super Administrator you will receive e-mail from your homepage.

Admin password: Mambo suggests a password. You can accept it or create a similarly complicated password. A simple one would be sufficient for a local installation.

Accept the default options in the File Permissions and Directory Permissions dialog. During installation, Mambo automatically sets access rights to those parts of the system where files are uploaded or programs are installed.

Step 4

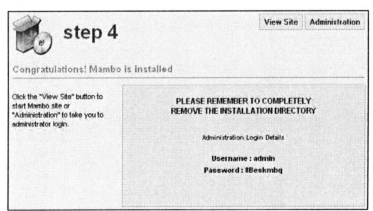

Figure 2.16: Successful Installation

The fourth and final step congratulates you on a successful installation.

There is a notice in bold, red text that prompts you to delete the installation directory. Take good heed of this notice, because your Mambo website will not run if you don't delete the directory.

In addition, your Administration Login Details are indicated. Note down the username and password.

> Mambo assigns a new password when you go backwards from step 4, for instance, if you want to change your settings or if the installation wasn't quite successful. If you have forgotten or mislaid the administrator password, there is a solution in the Appendix.

The installation is now complete. You have a choice between View Site (to start your homepage) and Administration (administration interface). To take a look at your newly created homepage, click on View Site. If you haven't deleted the installation directory as of yet, you will get a friendly reminder to delete it and to check out your page after you've done that.

Figure 2.17: Homepage After Installation

The result is very impressive. Look it over at your own pace, click on a few options, and try to orient yourself. Lot of Mambo's functionalities are used on this homepage, which is loaded with example data. We will take a good look at these.

3

A Tour of Your New Homepage

Now that you have installed your homepage and carefully explored it, we can take a look at the result together. At first glance, these pages look a bit confusing. In principle, they are divided into a frontend and a backend. Customers and web surfers see the frontend; the backend is only accessible by coworkers and/or administrators.

3.1 Frontend

After spending some time on the homepage, you will realize that many different functions are integrated into the page. In order to get a better overview, I have marked and labeled the different areas of the page, illustrated in Figure 3.1 overleaf.

The art of web design now consists of recognizing the elements that are important for your homepage, omitting the unimportant ones, and presenting it to the user in a logical, easy-to-understand, and attractive format. The result is always a compromise between functionality and organization.

From the configuration, this structure reminds one of a daily newspaper or a portal like Yahoo! or Freenet. On the left and right there are boxes with clearly defined contents. In the centre are announcements.

A so-called template determines the layout of the page. **Templates** are exchangeable and modifiable, meaning that the same content can be displayed in different layouts. Every daily newspaper would envy you for this functionality. Let's go over the example layout a bit more closely.

There are five different categories of areas on the page:

- Menus
- Content
- Advertising
- Functions
- Decorative Elements

3.1.1 Menus

Menus are there to make navigation on the page as easy as possible for the user. There are different menus for different tasks. Mambo has four kinds of menus in the example data. You can add as many additional menus as you want. The fourth menu, by the way, is not shown in our example. The registered user sees the so-called user menu after he or she has logged on.

Figure 3.1: Structure of the Homepage

Top Menu

The **top menu** is as high up on the page as possible. It gives the user quick access to the most important content of the page. Such a menu often displays products, contacts, and company information:

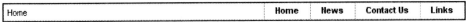

Home		Home	News	Contact Us	Links

Figure 3.2: Top Menu

Main Menu

The **main menu** is the central navigation area of the page. There should always be a link to return to the first page. This menu should appear in exactly the same position on every page of the website. The main menu is an important orientation place for the user:

Figure 3.3: Main Menu

Other Menu

An additional menu, the **other menu** can pop up in all kinds of places (module positions). Depending on the content and context of the page it can make sense to offer additional menu options:

Figure 3.4: Other Menu

3.1.2 Content

Finally the content that we want to manage is here!

What is Content

Content can be a message, an editorial article, or a static page with explanations. Content can be also a dynamic link directory (http://www.google.com/), a shop (http://dell.com/), or a flea market (http://www.ebay.com/).

Content can also be something completely dynamic and open to everybody. The free encyclopedia Wikipedia (http://www.wikipedia.org/), for example, uses a content administration system that allows everyone to change the content. This special form of content administration is called **wiki** (http://en.wikipedia.org/wiki/Wiki). Everyone can change and even delete content. So far it is working amazingly well.

The opposite of wiki is static content, which once written, is valid for a long time. For example, take this book. It will become outdated regarding the version numbers of the software discussed, although it has the advantage of explaining and illuminating the topic comprehensively in that connection, at present. I produce content in a certain format and therefore operate a type of content management.

Folders, flyers, stickers, business reports, and manuals are also usually of static nature. Created for a certain event, after some time they become outdated or simply wrong.

Many older web pages consist exclusively of static elements. On the Internet, however, the clock ticks a little faster. That which is complaisantly tolerated with books, folders, and other printed materials (after all, I can also read the book at the beach and in the subway), is regarded to be a serious shortcoming by visitors to your website. Nothing is worse for the image of your company than a four-year old static website with a button announcing "Powered by...", which refers to hopelessly outdated software.

The presentational possibilities of content are inexhaustible. They depend on the available terminal, bandwidth, and many other things that are in turn dependent on the user. The user of the message plays an increasingly important role. Who actually forms your target group?

A platitude says, "Content is king!"

It depends on the content. Every web agency would now probably crack a smile and get on with the daily job of creating the next website. Millions of dollars in advertising budgets for products such as frozen spinach or beer are proof of the fact that successful communication also works without unique content. The statement that content is crucial, is, however, fundamentally correct. If you have nothing to say or nothing to offer, nobody will listen to you of his or her own free will. Since you probably don't have a million-dollar advertising budget, you also can't force people to do it. No matter how beautiful websites without content may look, or how many terminals may display them, nobody will voluntarily visit them.

First Page/Front Page

Content is announced on the first page of the website, as illustrated in Figure 3.5. Content has an author, a date of preparation, a heading, a hook, and perhaps a picture. The hook is to make the visitor curious and to get him or her to click on a Read more link in order to read the entire message:

Figure 3.5: Front Page

The Latest Messages/The Most Often Read Messages

The message can be displayed in different formats. People are usually interested in the *newest* and in what *others* are reading as illustrated in Figure 3.6:

LATEST NEWS	POPULAR
■ Newsflash 1	■ Example FAQ Item 2
■ Newsflash 2	■ Example FAQ Item 1
■ Newsflash 3	■ Example News Item 4
■ Example News Item 2	■ Example News Item 1
■ Example News Item 1	■ Example News Item 2

Figure 3.6: The Latest Messages/The Most Often Read Messages

Because of that, our example layout has an appropriate area within which the last five messages are always displayed, and another area where the most read messages are announced. This second area is possible, because Mambo logs each hit on a message in the database and tracks the number of times it has been accessed.

Plan the content of your site carefully! Everyone in the world can read it and use it against you in cases of doubt. You could become the victim of a litigation lawyer, disappointed colleagues, or other unpleasantries.

On the other hand this has an unbeatable advantage: Everyone in the world can read your content, add his or her opinion to it, and contact you. What an opportunity!

You should be aware of both of these directions when you conceptualize content.

3.1.3 Advertising

When your site becomes popular and if the content is right, you can sell advertising space. Advertising space usually means banner links.

Banners are small graphics (in .gif, .jpg, .png, or .swf format) that induce the visitor to leave your website via a single click on the banner. If you really want that, look for a space in your layout and consider using it for advertising.

Banner Area

The size of the banner area is determined by the current banners. In our case this is 468 x 60 pixels as illustrated in Figure 3.7:

Figure 3.7: Banner Area

3.1.4 Functions

Functions are elements needed to make interactivity possible. In Mambo these functions are called **modules**. A module is something that takes up space on the web page and fulfils a certain function.

Login Area

A **login module** is important if you want to separate your website into a public and a protected area. The visitor then has to have a way of registering and of logging on. Perhaps he or she even occasionally forgets his or her password. The login module should be able to take all situations into consideration as illustrated in Figure 3.8:

Figure 3.8: Login Module

Polling

Since our content is designed for certain target groups, we should now and then ask the group that actually surfs our site for their opinion. This is the simplest way of getting utilizable opinions about your site.

Mambo has integrated a survey component, whose display module is on the example page as illustrated in Figure 3.9:

Figure 3.9: Survey Module

Who is Online

This module is about communication and community. After the user has been able to see which messages are recent and particularly popular, naturally he or she would like to know who is navigating the site right now. In this case a distinction is made between guests and logged on users as illustrated in Figure 3.10:

Figure 3.10: Who is Online?

Feeds

News feeds are becoming more and more popular. These are standardized collections of content, which can be processed further—the content of your site, without the dead weight of the rest of the website. The syndication module (Figure 3.11) offers the most diverse feeds:

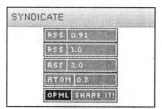

Figure 3.11: Syndication Module

You will learn more about this technology in Section 4.7.7.

> Deliberate carefully whether you want to offer such features on your website. If you claim in your content that you are the largest website in U.S. and only one guest cavorts on your site, it will hurt your credibility. But if you do indeed constantly have 10-20 visitors and logged on users, then this is a good way to demonstrate dynamics.

Back

Back is a small word of great importance and forms a giant portion of user friendliness. After one has pressed on a link, sometimes it is not at all easy to return exactly to the spot where one was just before. The Back button tries to make that possible:

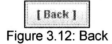
Figure 3.12: Back

Search Field

Similar to the Back button, the Search field also contributes greatly to the user friendliness of a website. Many pages have search fields. Often, however, the programs behind the search field don't scan the entire content of the page. With Mambo, however, all pages are definitely scanned:

Figure 3.13: Search Field

You can type a search term and press *Enter* on the keyboard. The result is a hit list, with the desired term visually emphasized.

3.1.5 Decorative Elements

After so many functions, modules, and contents, the issue of design, corporate identity, and the *look* and *feel* of the website pops up.

A **template** represents the layout of the page and is laid on top of the content like a screen. Since it is hard to argue either about taste or beauty, you have the option of providing different templates for the same content. For example, the look of your website in winter could be different than that in summer, or it could have a baseball look during the World Series. Chapter 6 deals with the creation of your own templates.

In principle, a template consists of one or more logos, a certain color combination, selected character fonts and sizes, and as clever an arrangement of the available content as possible. There are two logos (Figure 3.14) and a footer line (Figure 3.15) in the example template:

Figure 3.14: Logo 1, Logo 2

Copyright 2000 - 2005 Miro International Pty Ltd. All rights reserved.
Mambo is Free Software released under the GNU/GPL License.

Figure 3.15: Footer

3.1.6 Prospects

After this tour and from your own experience, I am sure you can understand that the administration of contents can be a very demanding task. Above all, it is important not to lose sight of the overview.

3.2 Backend

The administration of the website takes place in the backend with the name *Mambo administration*. You can reach the Mambo administration under the URL [Domain name]/administrator/.

If you are working with a local installation, the URL is

http://localhost/mambo/administrator/

Log on with your admin ID as shown in Figure 3.16.

You have specified the user data yourself in the web installer during installation.

You will see an interface with menus, icons, and tabs, identical to the graphic interface of your operating system, as illustrated in Figure 3.17:

Figure 3.16: Mambo Administration—Login

Figure 3.17: Mambo Administration

In a working environment you should, for security purposes, protect the directory [mambo]/administrator/ with a .htaccess file. Because of the widespread use of Mambo, the first successful hacker attempt at the administration is expected.

4
Customizing Mambo

Customizing means the adaptation of a standard program to the needs of the user. In our case, you are the user and the standard program is Mambo Open Source, or more exactly the frontend of your Mambo installation.

In the Mambo administration (referred to in Chapter 3), you can adapt your site, make changes, and fill it with content.

Typically, the first two things that the owners of a site want to do are to adjust the language to the native language and to change the colors and layouts. So, we will first discuss these two things.

4.1 The First Attempt

In case you want to reach a native target group with your site, you should understand the language of the target group and build the site in that language. If you want to address an international audience, you should use English as the standard language. Regardless of which language you choose, you need a customized language file. As a base, it's best to take what is already available.

4.1.1 Installation of a Different Language File

For example, if you want to reach a German target group, download the `m4.5.2_germani.zip` and `m4.5.2_germanf.zip` files. The **i** stands for informal and **f** for formal language.

Log on to Mambo administration as described earlier and click Site | Language Manager | Install as shown in Figure 4.1:

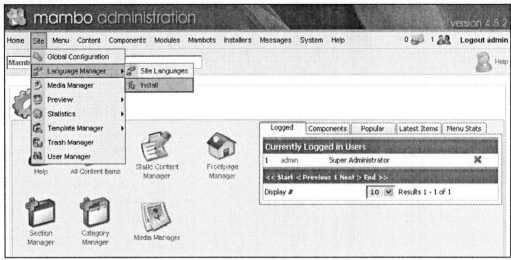

Figure 4.1: Language File Installation

Now click Browse and select the m4.5.2_germanf.zip file. Click Upload File & Install. If all rights are correctly set, you will receive the message:

Upload language – Success

After one click on the Continue link, you will see the available languages. Besides English there is also 'German formal-you (Sie)' and a bit of information about the creator of the language file. In the other ZIP archive is the German version with the 'familiar-you (Du)' way of addressing. If you want, you can install this version as well.

The green checkmark for the standard language, however, is still for English. If you want to select the German option, click Publish, which is on the right, above the Language Manager. The icons that finalize actions and dialogs are always in this position:

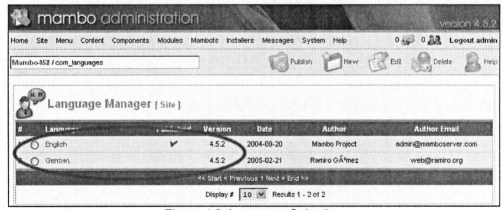

Figure 4.2: Language Selection

4.1.2 Translation of a Menu Entry

Your frontend now speaks German. Go to `http://localhost/mambo/` and take a good look at the search field and the login module. Click the Search link in the main menu.

This page displays both German and English languages. Everything that is programmed to function automatically, like the search procedure or the login procedure, is in German; everything else is in English.

Why? The answer is quite simple. Only the words and sentences that are programmed in can be translated. A large part of the page, however, consists of entered content. This content appears in the language in which it was entered. In our case, the sample data was provided in English.

Before you try to translate the sample page, look at the buttons in the Language Manager. Besides Publish, there are New, Edit, Delete, and Help. Mambo's online help can be accessed by clicking the Help button.

With the New button you can install new language packages and with Delete you can erase them. But the Edit button is really interesting. Select the language that you want to see and click Edit. The Language Editor opens and you can make changes online, as shown in Figure 4.3:

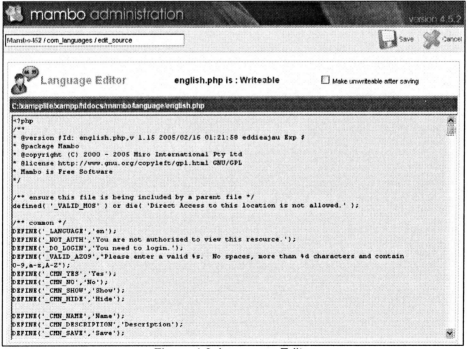

Figure 4.3: Language Editor

Browse through the language file for a while. You will get a feel of the Mambo functions by doing this.

At present, the language file is *writable*, thus alterable from PHP or any other tool. If you are of the opinion that the translation was successful and you want more security, simply mark the appropriate check box to make the file read only. The write rights are now revoked for this file and granted next time for memory procedures only. In order to restore the original rights situation, you have to change the file rights from your FTP client or from a shell with the command chmod. Click Save or Cancel if you wish to exit the Language Editor.

What do you have to do in order to change the menu entry Search into Suchen or to rename the Main Menu into Hauptmenü?

Exit the Language Editor and click Menu | mainmenu. You are now in the Menu Manager. Click the Search link as shown in Figure 4.4 and edit it in the form that appears on your monitor as shown in Figure 4.5:

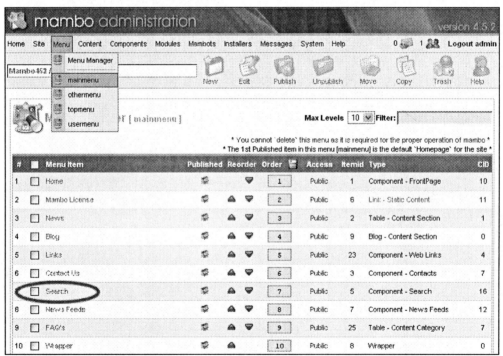

Figure 4.4: Menu Manager

Don't worry yet about the numerous configuration options; simply replace the word Search with Suche and click Apply. You will now see Suche on the Main Menu of your site!

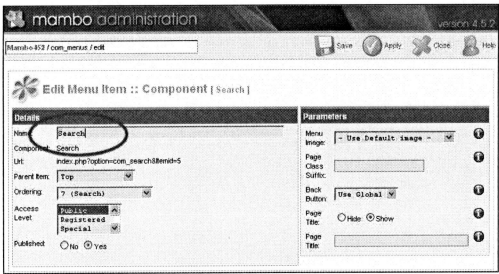

Figure 4.5: Change Item Menu

4.1.3 Modifying the Menu Name

In order to make a Hauptmenü from the Main Menu, open the Module Manager by clicking Modules | Site Modules (Figure 4.6). Click on the Main Menu link to get a form, just like with the menu entry. Change the text and the Main Menu becomes a Hauptmenü:

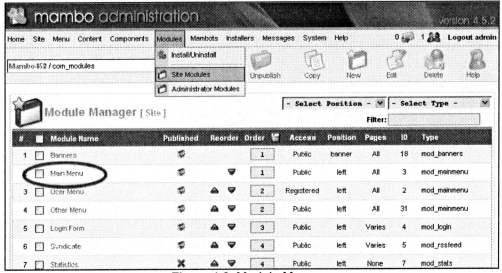

Figure 4.6: Module Manager

4.1.4 Changing the Template for Your Site

Now that everything looks a bit more familiar, you may want your site to have a completely different design. In order to see what is included in Mambo as standard, switch to Site | Template Manager | Site Templates in the Template Manager (Figure 4.7). "Site" means your website, that is, the frontend. As you can see, there are administrator templates:

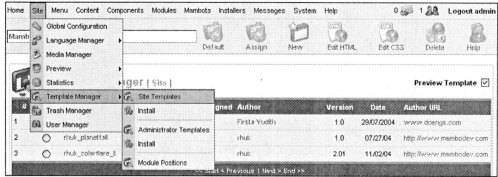

Figure 4.7: Template Manager

Three finished templates are included with Mambo. The currently active template is marked with a green checkmark.

If you slide your mouse over the name of the template, a small thumbnail view appears, as shown in Figure 4.8. To assign this template to your site, select the radio button before the name of the desired template and click Default in the menu bar. Switch to your site and click the Update button in the browser:

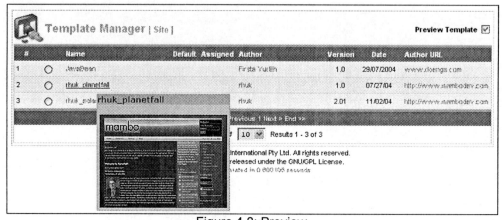

Figure 4.8: Preview

You have a different layout and a completely new appearance. The menus, for example, are on the right side, and in addition have the German translations Hauptmenü and Suche. After this first round of satisfying our urge to play, we now get to some more elaborate customizing.

4.2 Configuration of Mambo Administration

Mambo offers nearly the same comfort level as any program with a graphical user interface, such as Windows, KDE, Gnome, or Aqua (Mac OS X). This is not self-evident for web pages and is made possible by the generous use of JavaScript. JavaScript is executed locally on your computer and can be deactivated in the browser. If this is done, you can no longer work with Mambo administration. Browsers, however, have been able to deal with JavaScript quite well for several years now and there aren't any serious security concerns any more. For this reason, you should enable JavaScript. In this context, I would highly recommend the open source Mozilla Firefox browser (http://www.mozilla.org). It is more secure and easier to use than Internet Explorer.

Figure 4.9: A Different Template

The Mambo administration, just like your site, consists of different elements.

In the top menu bar are the menus and on the right side are two notifications about whether you have received messages and how many users are logged on right now.

Below that is a field with a link that has information about which components are applicable to the currently shown manager (**infobar**). On the extreme right is the toolbar with various dimmed icons which are dependant on the manager.

If you slide your mouse over one of these icons, it lights up. You can click the left mouse button and implement the appropriate function:

Toolbar element	Relevance
Publish	The chosen element is published.
Unpublish	The chosen element is hidden from view.
Archive	The chosen element is moved to the archive.
New/New Item	The creation of a new element (link, contact, and message) is started.
Edit	The chosen element is loaded into the edit module.
Delete/Remove	The chosen element is deleted.
Trash	The chosen element is put in the trash container.
Restore/Untrash	The chosen element is retrieved from the trash container.
Move	The chosen element is moved to another section or category.
Copy	The chosen element is copied to another section or category.
Save	The chosen element is saved and the dialog is closed.
Apply	The changes are saved and the dialog remains open.
Cancel	The function being worked on is ended without any changes being saved.
Preview	The chosen element is shown in a preview window.
Upload	The chosen file is uploaded to the server.

Toolbar element	Relevance
Create	A subdirectory is created on the server.
Help	Mambo online help function is available.
Default	The chosen element becomes the default.
Assign	The chosen element is assigned to another element.

Table 4.1: Toolbar Elements

Under the toolbar is the workspace of the current manager. As shown in Figure 4.10 this is the Control Panel. It is displayed after logging in and offers quick access to the most important elements. If you do not see the Control Panel, simply click Home at the top-left corner in the menu bar:

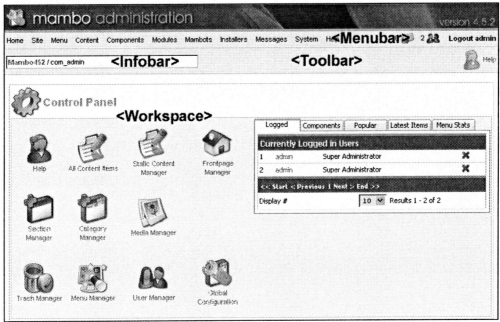

Figure 4.10: Mambo Administration

On the left, there are icons that refer to various managers. On the right, you find five tabs that give you an overview of the current status of your site. In the lower area you see a navigation bar that extends right across Mambo. Here you can set the number of lines displayed and navigate through the table if say 600 users are online at the same time.

This number is quite realistic with well-frequented Mambo sites. Changing the number of lines displayed is possible with all table displays.

Logged gives an overview of the currently logged in users. As administrator, by clicking on the red cross (x) next to the user name, you can log the user out.

Components shows the currently installed software components. If these have several options (for example, web links), then this component is represented as a heading with subpoints.

Popular tells you about the most surfed pages of your site. By clicking the page name, you switch to the Content Manager and see the respective page in editing mode. If you are in edit mode, you have to terminate the function with Cancel or Save and subsequently click Home to get back to the Control Panel.

Latest Items is similar to Popular. Here the content is shown in reverse chronological order. One click on the name also switches you to the Content Manager.

Menu Stats displays the number of menu elements in each menu.

The menu bar consists of eleven options. On the far left is the Home link that sends you back to the Control Panel. On the far right you can see the Help link.

You can configure the Control Panel by clicking Modules | Administrator Modules.

4.3 Help Menu

A call for help often resounds when you are immersed in work! With Help, Open Source differs drastically from other licensed program products. If you need assistance, you can ask or check the online archives of developers and users. If you have the necessary experience, you can even check the source code directly.

You will find an overview of the important items in the Help menu. This menu includes:

- A glossary
- An introduction to the people behind Mambo (*credits*)
- Tips for finding help on the net (*support*). Check http://forum. mamboserver.com, for answers to your questions
- http://help.mamboserver.com as the online help system for Mambo
- System information that allows you to check under which conditions your Mambo installation will work

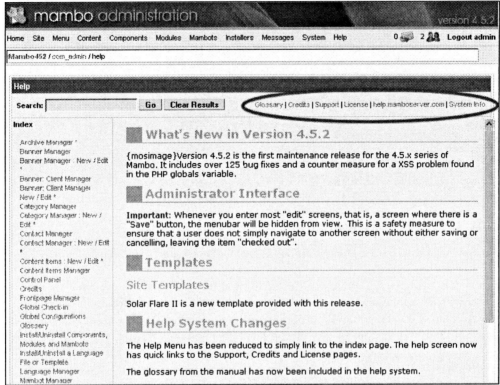

Figure 4.11: Mambo Online Help

On the left side of the page is a keyword list, behind which the respective help texts hide as shown in Figure 4.11. Before you post questions in the forum, please look at these help files and the posts in the forum contributions of others!

The Mambo Help work area is divided into three sections. On the top there is a search field and a bar with links as shown in Figure 4.11. On the left is an index of the available help texts and on the right is the main display area. By default, anything new about Mambo 4.5.2 is displayed in this space. All but two links refer to the server http://help.mamboserver.com/. In order to use this search, you have to be connected to the Internet. You *have* to do this unless you are working with a local version. Two other links refer to the text of the GNU Public License and to system information about your server as illustrated in Figure 4.12. This information is divided into three tabs:

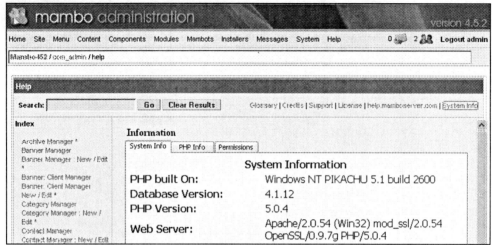

Figure 4.12: System Information

System Info displays a summary of the most important data. Right now I am working locally with Windows and the xampplite environment (for the installation procedure, refer to Chapter 2). Therefore I'm running very up-to-date software versions (Apache 2.0.53 and PHP 5.03), compared with the servers rented on the Internet.

PHP Info displays all information from the phpinfo() function. This is the complete configuration of the PHP interpreter.

Permissions displays the rights of your subdirectories. In order for Mambo to run error-free, all directories must be writable.

4.4 Site Menu

There are settings that apply to all individual pages and to your server. All of these settings are summarized in the Site menu.

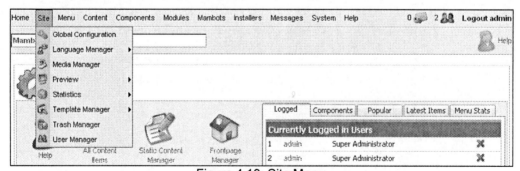

Figure 4.13: Site Menu

4.4.1 Site: Global Configuration

The global configuration workspace administers changes in the configuration.php file. In it are vitally important pieces of information, like the access details for the database server. This workspace is divided into ten tabs:

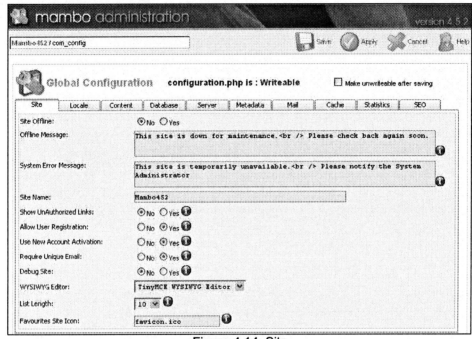

Figure 4.14: Site

Site

Site Offline: If, for instance, you are carrying out changes to your site and you don't want visitors to track your development progess, you can turn off your site.

Offline Message: The text entered here is displayed on your site when it is switched off. If you want to use another logo, you can save one with the name of [mambo]/images/logo.png. Otherwise, you have to customize the path accordingly.

Figure 4.15: Display notice when
the site is switched off

System Error Message: Here you can type in a message that is displayed if no connection can be established with the database server.

Site Name: This is the name of the page that you entered during the installation.

Show UnAuthorized Links: You have the ability to display individual pages only to registered users. It is possible that these pages get linked from a public connection. If you choose Yes, these links are displayed. When a visitor who has not logged on clicks on such a link, a message appears announcing that this is a protected area that requires registration.

Allow User Registration: Here you can select whether you want to permit users to do their own registration or not. If you operate a company site, you could set up user accounts for your coworkers, but forbid them to create their own account. With a community site, on the other hand, it is desirable for users to log themselves on.

Use New Account Activation: In order to protect yourself from automated programs that can create 20,000 user accounts on your site, you can ask for separate activation. The user gets an automatic e-mail sent to the address given by him or her. There is a link in this e-mail that activates the account. After activation he/she can log on normally.

Require Unique Email: Choose whether each e-mail address is to be used for one account only.

Debug Site: Here you can switch the site into debug mode. After activating this function, the database queries of the site are displayed. In order to generate a single Mambo page, 79 database queries are required, as shown in Figure 4.16:

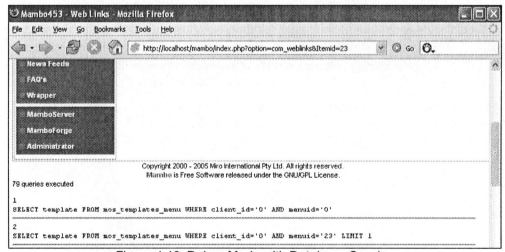

Figure 4.16: Debug Mode with Database Queries

WYSIWYG Editor: WYSIWYG is the abbreviation for "What you see is what you get" which means, "This is what you wanted, here it is!" The term originated at the beginning of graphic user interfaces, when it first became possible to see how the printed document would look as you typed the text into your word processor.

On the Internet, you normally fill out forms with no formatting ability. Formatting is done by HTML tags or program-specific mnemonics. A WYSIWYG editor is user-friendly, since you have to click an appropriate icon, just as when formatting text. This editor is automatically invoked for the text fields that require formatting as illustrated in Figure 4.17. It works with all the usual browsers:

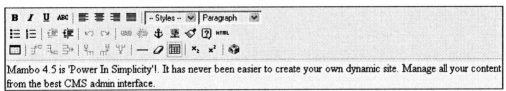

Figure 4.17: WYSIWYG Editor

Mambo also offers the ability of integrating other HTML editors. The default editor TinyMCE is used at this time. You can find out more about it from `http://tinymce.moxiecode.com/`.

List Length: Lists, like news and links, will crop up every now and then on your site. With this, you can set the default number of entries that such a list can have.

Favorites Site Icon: Every site can offer the surfer a so-called **favorite-site icon** (**favicon**). This small picture is displayed to the left of the URL, as well as in the bookmarks of the browser. This works really well in most browsers:

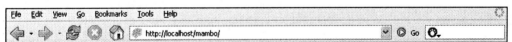

Figure 4.18: Favicon in Firefox

In Internet Explorer, however, this works only under certain conditions (compare Figure 4.18 and Figure 4.19):

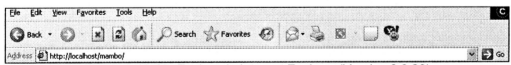

Figure 4.19: No Favicon in Internet Explorer (Version 6.0.29)

The icons have to be available in a certain format. You can specify the name for the icon. You will find the file in the main directory of Mambo. You can create icons using an icon editor such as SnIco Edit (http://www.snidesoft.com/staticpages/index.php ?page=20050504142037205).

Locale

With this tab you can localize your page as illustrated in Figure 4.20. By localization, one means adaptation to country-specific conventions. The options available are:

Language: Here you specify the language of the site. All available languages are indicated in the option drop-down menu. Section 4.1.1 discusses how to install new language packages.

Time Offset: This setting can be used to display the correct time; for example, if the server that Mambo runs on is located in the USA, but the site is meant for visitors in Germany.

Country Locale: Every country has certain defaults for the display of numbers and dates (http://en.wikipedia.org/wiki/Locale). With this option, you can specify the format. PHP offers the ability of implementing different functions depending on the mnemonic entered as *locale*. The approach is sound; however, this does not always work when creating a template.

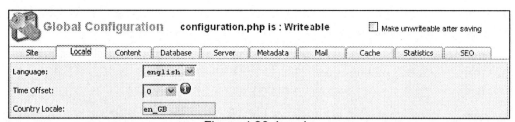

Figure 4.20: Locale

Content

The settings for the content display of the entire site are set here. You may set your preferred settings in the following options:

Linked Titles: Here you can set the title of a content element to be shown as a link. This link then refers to the same target, as the Read More link.

Read More Link: A lot of content consists of a hook (*intro text*) and the actual text. Here you decide whether you want to have a Read More link under the hook, which refers to the complete text:

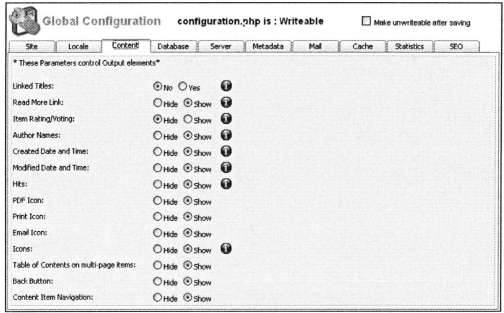

Figure 4.21: Content

Item Rating/Voting: This lets your visitors evaluate the contents of the site. If you click Show, an evaluation component is displayed above the item (see Figure 4.22).

Author Names: Is the name of the author of the content to be displayed? If you select Show, then the name of the author appears above the article as shown in Figure 4.22:

Figure 4.22: Author Name

Created Date and Time: Should the date and time of creation of content be displayed? If you select Show, text such as Wednesday, 12 May 2004 is written above the article as shown in Figure 4.22.

Modified Date and Time: Should the date and time of modification of content be displayed? If you select Show, Last Updated (Wednesday, 07 July 2004) is displayed under the text, as illustrated in Figure 4.22.

Hits: Here you decide whether to display the number of hits on a content item:

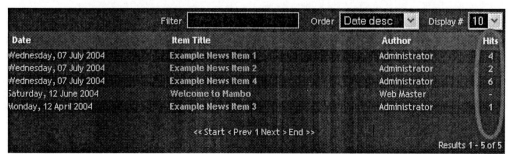

Figure 4.23: News List with Hits

PDF Icon: Should a PDF icon be displayed above the content (see Figure 4.22)? After clicking this icon, your content is prepared as a PDF file! In order to view the PDF file, you need the free Acrobat Reader (http://www.adobe.com/products/acrobat/).

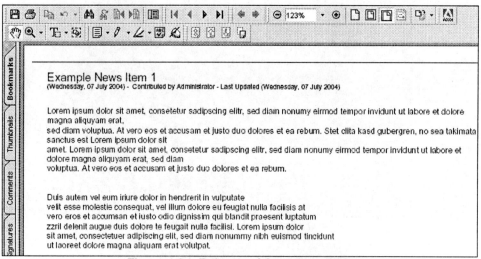

Figure 4.24: Release of Content in PDF

Print Icon: Here you can determine whether a print icon is to be displayed above the content (see Figure 4.22). After clicking this icon, the content is prepared for printing.

E-mail Icon: Should an e-mail icon be displayed above the content? After clicking this icon, a form is displayed that allows you to send a reference about this content to somebody else, as illustrated in Figure 4.25:

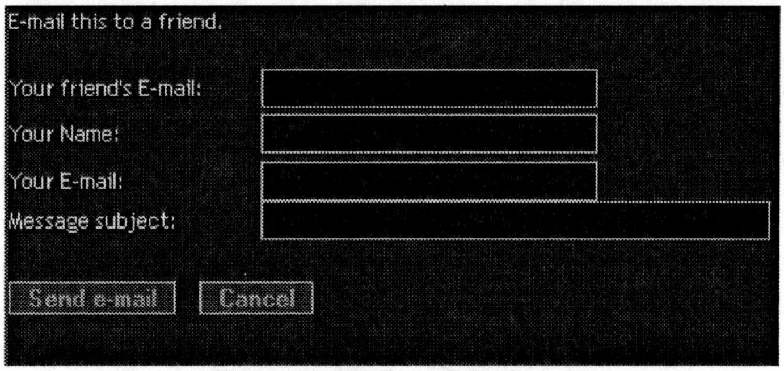

Figure 4.25: E-mail Referral

Icons: Here you decide whether to show PDF, print, and e-mail as icons or as links.

Table of Contents on multi-page items: It is possible to write content that covers several pages. For that, a Mambot is contained in the text. We will discuss Mambot in greater detail in Chapter 7. If you select Show, a table of contents is automatically produced for this piece of content.

Back Button: Do you want a Back button on every page?

Content Item Navigation: If you select Show here, a bar with the buttons Next and Previous is placed under the content, with which you can navigate through items.

Database
In this tab, you can see the access information for your MySQL server:

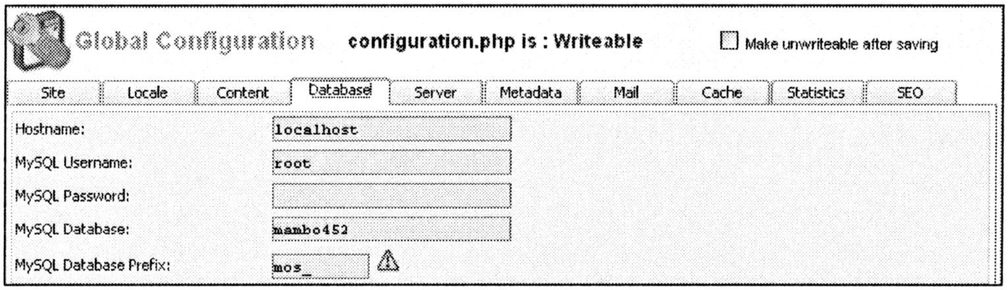

Figure 4.26: Database

Server

In the server section you'll find more information about settings that you can change:

Figure 4.27: Server

Absolute Path: The absolute path on your server is the path from the root directory of the server to your Mambo installation. On a local machine running under Windows, for example, it is C:/xampplite/xampp/htdocs/mambo; on a Linux server however, it is /is/htdocs/wp1007226_40G0RIWV3E/www.

Live Site: The Live Site is the URL by which the site is accessible on the Internet.

Secret Word: This is the encoded administrator password. Refer to the Appendix to find out what to do if you forget your admin password.

GZIP Page Compression: With this you can enable compression of the pages. If the browser and web server support this function, the pages are delivered in ZIP format and unpacked by the client browser. This can substantially increase the speed of page download, especially with slow Internet connections.

Login Session Lifetime: If you log on as a user, you produce a so-called session. Unless you log yourself out, this session is deleted after the number of seconds that you set here.

Error Reporting: With these switches, PHP's own error reporting mechanism is activated.

Option	Description
System Default	Here the settings from the configuration file php.ini are used.
None	Errors are not logged.

Option	Description
Simple	Errors and warnings are logged. This setting corresponds to the parameter `error_reporting` (`E_ERROR`|`E_WARNING`|`E_PARSE`)
Maximum	Errors, warnings, and references are logged. This setting corresponds to the parameter `error_reporting` (`E_ALL`)

Table 4.2: Error Reporting

Help Server: Here you can register another URL for the Mambo help server.

File Creation: If files on the server are created by Mambo, the standard rights set up on the server are applied to these files. These settings are usually sufficient. If you have problems with uploads, select the second option and overwrite the server settings.

Directory Creation: The setup options described for files (refer to *File Creation*) also applies to directories.

Metadata

Metadata is data about data, for example a description of your site. Metadata plays a role with search engines. How large this role is, is however disputed. Nevertheless, metadata represents a good way to describe your site in short and concise words. If you look at the HTML source code of a Mambo page, you can see the following metatags in the upper area:

```
<meta name="description" content="Mambo - the dynamic portal engine
and content management system" />
<meta name="keywords" content="mambo, Mambo" />
```

Here you can set default values as shown below:

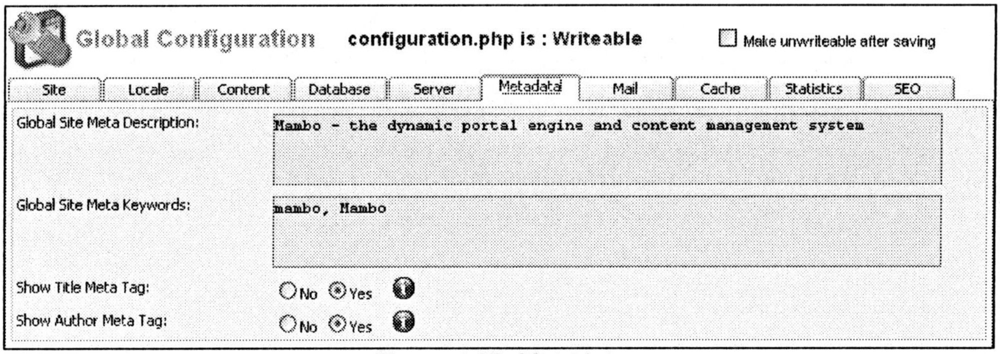

Figure 4.28: Metadata

Global Site Meta Description: This description of site content is often displayed as the result by search engines. One should therefore pay special attention to this tag, because it is on the basis of this information that the surfer decides whether to visit your site or not.

Global Site Meta Keywords: Keywords are the most important words in a document. They should describe the main purpose of your site. Some search engines particularly favor the keywords. Individual words are separated by commas and several words can be included between two commas with normal blanks.

The keywords should be limited to a maximum of 1,000, as more than that are not selected. Note that the use of fewer key words helps each individual word get a higher priority in the search engine. Deliberate about which the most often used keywords are and which are likely to be searched for most.

Show Title Meta Tag: With individual content pages, the content title is blended in as a metatag.

Show Author Meta Tag: With individual content pages, the author's name is blended in as a metatag.

Mail

Under this tab, you can decide the methods for sending Mambo mail, as shown below:

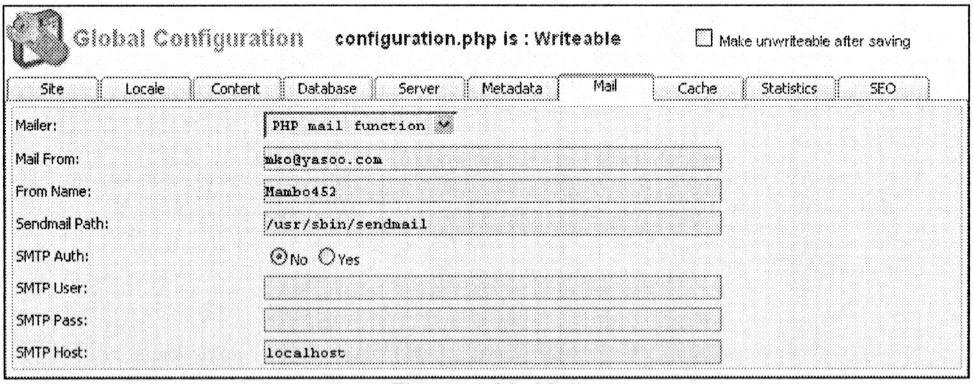

Figure 4.29: Mail

Mailer: Here you can select whether you want to use the PHP mail function, Sendmail, or another e-mail account, for example, Yahoo or GMX.

Mail From: For mail generated by Mambo, this e-mail address is automatically displayed as the sender.

From Name: This name is automatically displayed as the sender for mail generated by Mambo.

Sendmail Path: If, instead of the PHP mail function, you want to use the Sendmail program that is presumably available to all Linux servers, you have to enter the path to the program in this textbox.

SMTP Auth: Chose whether you want to use an external mail server.

SMTP User: This is your user name for this e-mail provider.

SMTP Pass: This is your password for this e-mail provider.

SMTP Host: This is the SMTP server of this e-mail provider.

Cache

A cache is a temporary storage facility. Your browser, for example, has a picture cache, which makes pictures already downloaded available faster:

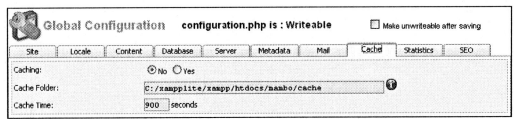

Figure 4.30: Cache

Mambo uses a similar mechanism on the server to cache pages generated by PHP. This option can drastically reduce response time with frequently visited pages.

Statistics

Here, you can enable or disable the statistics functions for your site:

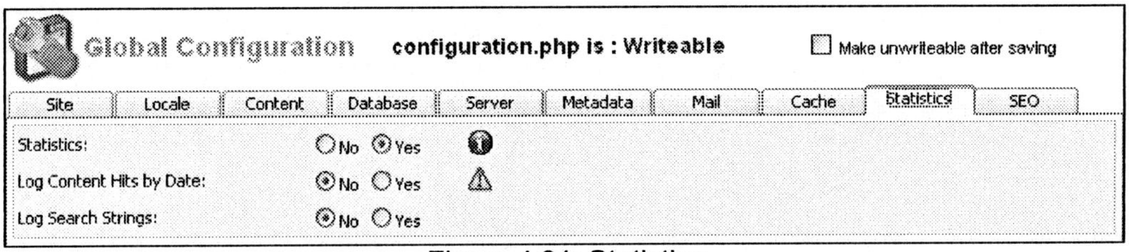

Figure 4.31: Statistics

Statistics: Here you determine whether or not to produce statistics.

Log Content Hits by Date: Here you enable daily-updated content statistics. Not just the complete page accesses, but hits on individual elements of an HTML page are also tracked here. Unfortunately, there is still no analysis program for this data at this time. By the way, very large data sets are produced within a very short time.

Log Search Strings: This switch can give very interesting results. It collects words that visitors to your site enter into the search field.

SEO (Search Engine Optimization)

This subject is about search engine-friendly URLs. Normally a URL of a content management system looks like this:

`http://localhost/mambo/index.php?option=com_contact&Itemid=3`. Such URLs are not normally stored by search engines, since the search engine assumes that the content is constructed dynamically and will probably change soon.

Figure 4.32: SEO

Search Engine Friendly URLs: With this switch you can make a search engine-friendly URL from a dynamic URL. If you set the switch to Yes, links look something like this: `http://localhost/component/option,com_contact/Itemid,47/`.

The principle is based on a feature of the Apache web server. With its rewrite engine it can manipulate URLs at will. Besides the switch, you also have to rename the file `htaccess.txt` in the Mambo directory to `.htaccess`. With Windows, such a renaming is only possible with certain programs, for example, the Ultraedit editor. With Linux, the renaming function is problem-free; the file, however, is subsequently no longer displayed in its FTP client (depending on the server configuration). In addition, the provider may not permit `.htaccess` files, since they represent a security risk for the web server.

Dynamic Page Titles: No matter what, you should switch this to Yes. The title of your content is then displayed with the page name in the title bar of the browser window for each and every page access:

Figure 4.33: Dynamic Page Title

4.4.2 Site: Language Manager

You already know the Language Manager from our first walkthrough (see Section 4.1.1). Besides selecting languages for the site, you can also install new language files here. In our first attempt, we accomplished this by uploading the language file. Mambo, however, also allows you to load files onto the server via FTP and then to install them from the filesystem. The advantage with this is that you can install several language files in one processing step:

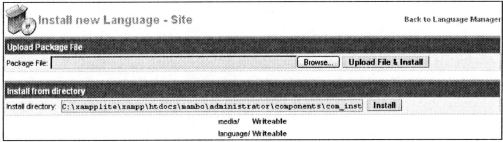

Figure 4.34: Install New Language

4.4.3 Site: Media Manager

You can think of the media manager as a file explorer or an FTP program in your operating system. With it, you can upload files with the extensions .gif, .png, .jpg, .bmp, .pdf, .swf, .doc, .xls, or .ppt into different directories and administer them.

This manager is extremely convenient, especially if you have administration rights, but no FTP access:

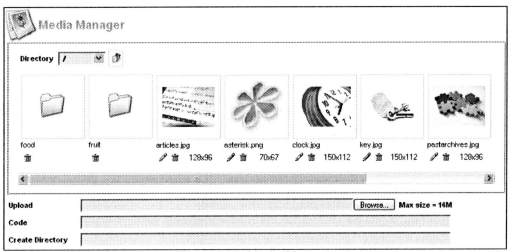

Figure 4.35: Media Manager

Directory: Select the desired directory, whose content is to be displayed.

Media Bar: This bar lists the files (media). Depending on the type of file, you will find more information about each below. A stylus icon and a trash can icon are displayed. With a click on the stylus you can create a complete HTML link, which you can then copy and paste into your content. If you click on the stylus of the Mambo logo, for instance, the Code field displays the following:

```
<img src="http://localhost/mambo/images/stories/asterisk.png"
align="left" hspace="6"
alt="asterisk.png" />
```

That is the HTML code to display a picture left justified with a border of 6 pixels.

Upload: Click Browse and select the desired file from your local hard drive. Subsequently, click the upload icon in the toolbar. The file is uploaded and displayed. Mambo uses media as it is. Remember that it is not a good idea to put a 3 MB picture from a digital camera on your web page in that size. On the Internet, pictures should be no larger than 50 KB. There are people who still do not have high-speed access to the Internet!

You should have the following times in the back of your mind as a ground rule for the download time for 100 KB (about the size of a portal web page with pictures):

Connection type	100 Kilobyte download
DSL	Depending on the configuration, less than a second!
ISDN	About 15 seconds.
Modem (56 kbps)	About 25 seconds.

Table 4.3: Time taken to download a 100 KB file

Create Directory: You can enter a name for a new subdirectory in this field. After clicking the create icon in the toolbar, the subdirectory is created and can be selected from the options list in the top area (directory).

4.4.4 Site: Preview

Here you get a preview of your site:

Figure 4.36: Preview

You have three options:

- In New Window: The preview is displayed in a new browser window.

- Inline: The preview is shown in the workspace, with scroll bars on the sides, if the page is too large to fit on the monitor.
- Inline with Positions: The preview is shown in the workspace, with markings for the individual module positions.

4.4.5 Site: Statistics

Here you can evaluate the statistical data, which you hopefully enabled in Section 4.4.1 on the Statistics tab as shown in Figure 4.37:

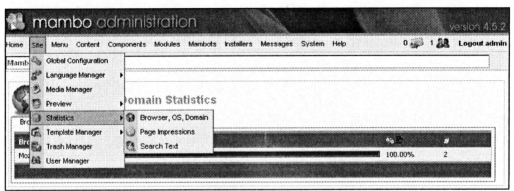

Figure 4.37: Statistics

Browser, OS, Domain: In this area you get three flags with information as to which browser, operating system, and domain has visited your site. This is based on the data that a browser supplies automatically to the web server. If, for example, Google visits your site with a program to incorporate your pages in its index, no information is transferred.

> The maximum upload size per file depends on the PHP configuration of your provider. In my case it is 16 MB. Larger files would have to be uploaded via FTP.

Page Impressions: Here you can see the individual pages, the creation date, and the number of hits.

Search Text: The search words entered by your visitors are tracked here.

4.4.6 Site: Template Manager

You are already familiar with the Template Manager from where we installed another template for the site in Section 4.1.4:

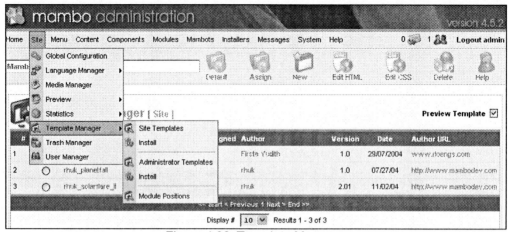

Figure 4.38: Template Manager

Site Templates

Here you can set up the templates for your site.

Default: Pick a template and click the default icon to use it as the default template for your site.

Assign: Select a template and click on assign to apply it to individual pages:

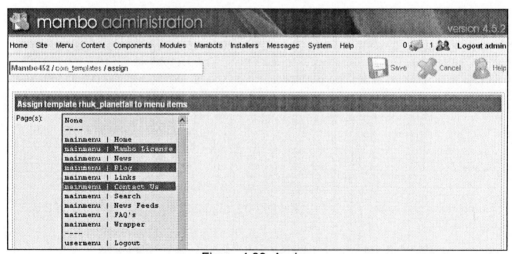

Figure 4.39: Assign

The existing menu elements are indicated to you. Mark the appropriate elements that you want to apply to the template. You can chose more than one by holding down the *Control* key while clicking on all desired elements one after the other.

New: Here you install a new template, like the language file from Section 4.1.1. There is a large selection of existing templates (http://www.mambohut.com/), which you can install either by means of an upload or via installation from a directory.

Edit HTML/Edit CSS: Here you can work directly on the HTML or CSS source code of the selected template (as shown in Figure 4.40). Templates always consist of an HTML and a CSS file:

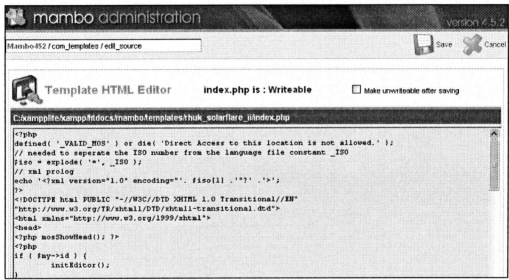

Figure 4.40: HTML Editor

I'm sure that seeing how a template is developed is interesting even for the beginner.

Delete: Here you can completely delete an installed template.

Install
This is the installation mask for site templates. You wind up here if you click New in Site Templates or if you come directly from the menu Site | Templates Manager | Install. You can install new template file packages by uploading or by doing a directory installation.

Administrator Templates
What applies to your site, naturally also applies to the administration interface. You can assign other templates and install new ones, just like with the site templates of your administration interface. Mambo includes two administrator templates that you can chose from.

Install
Just as with the site templates, you can also install administrator templates. You wind up here if you click New in administrator templates or if you come directly from the Site |

Templates | Install menu. New template file packages can be installed by uploading or by a directory installation.

Module Positions

Here the display positions of the modules of a template are administered. You can define up to 56 different positions. You can display module content in these positions (see also Section 4.8).

4.4.7 Site: Trash Manager

The Trash Manager contains your garbage bin. It collects content and menu elements that you have disposed of by clicking on the trash icon, and files it under two tabs:

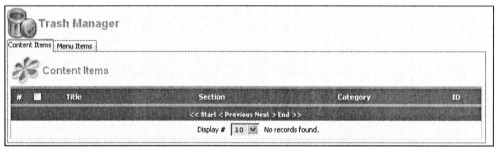

Figure 4.41: Trash Manager

You can retrieve items from the trash by selecting the element and clicking Restore; if you click Delete, it is irretrievably deleted.

> If you get involved in this, you have to know what you are doing.
> Knowledge of HTML and CSS is essential.

4.4.8 Site: User Manager

Users play a very special role on your Mambo site. At the moment, you are the only user (*admin*) that the Mambo administration knows. If you allow user registration on your site (see Section 4.4.1), presumably there will be a lot more very shortly.

In the User Manager (illustrated in Figure 4.42), you can change, delete, block, and assign different rights to users.

In the overview list you can see the real name of the user, if the user is logged in at the moment—symbolized by a green check mark (Logged In), if the user is activated (Enabled), the UserID, the Group, his or her e-mail address, and the date of his/her last access to your site. This refers to their last login to your site, not login to Mambo administration.

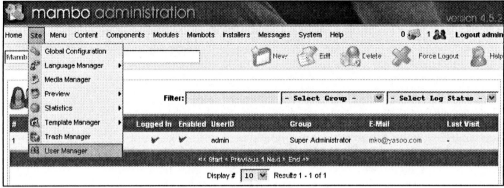
Figure 4.42: User Manager

New

With New you can create a new user. By clicking on New you get an appropriate form (Figure 4.43). The following options are available for you:

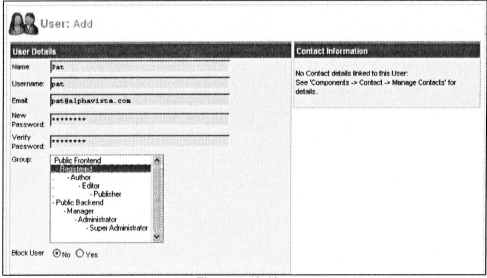
Figure 4.43: New

Name: The real name of the user.

Username: The user ID.

E-Mail: The e-mail address. Depending on the settings in the Site | Global Configuration menu, an e-mail address can be used just once or several times (see Section 4.4.1).

Password: The password has to be entered twice for verification.

Group: The group affiliation is divided into two large areas: Users that are only allowed to visit your *Public Frontend* (Table 4.4) and users that are allowed in the Mambo administration (*Public Administration*) (Table 4.5). All content in Mambo can be allotted to these groups.

Group	Rights
Registered	A registered user can log in and see some part of the site that the visitor cannot see.
Author	The author can see everything that a registered user can. An author can write information and modify his or her information. There is generally a link from the user menu for this.
Editor	The editor can do everything that an author can. An editor can write and change any information that appears in the front-end.
Publisher	The publisher can do everything that an editor can. A publisher can write information and change any information that appears in the front-end. In addition, a publisher can decide whether information is published or not.

Table 4.4: Front-end User Group

The backend user group consists of the Manager, Administrator, and Super Administrator:

Group	Rights
Manager	A manager can create content and can see various information about the system. He/she is not allowed to: Administer users Install modules and components Upgrade a user to super administrator or modify a super administrator Work on the menu option Site | Global Configuration Send a mass mailing to all users Change and/or install templates and language files
Administrator	An administrator is not allowed to: Upgrade a user to super administrator or modify a super administrator Work on the menu option Site | Global Configuration Send a mass mailing to all users Change and/or install templates and language files
Super Administrator	A super administrator can execute all functions in Mambo administration. Only a super administrator can create another super administrator.

Table 4.5: Backend User Groups

Block User: Here you can block a user and forbid him access.

Edit: With Edit you can modify a user.

Delete: Delete allows you to delete a user.

Force Logout: With Force Logout you can force the immediate logout of a user.

Special Users: A special user is any user that has more rights than an author. At the moment it is not possible to create your own user groups in Mambo. The group, special users, is helpful in limiting content elements to this group. That can be very helpful if, for example, one wants to offer links to internal help files only to these special users.

4.5 Menu: Menu Manager

The individual menus are administered here. Mambo has four different menus in the sample data (main menu, other menu, top menu, and user menu).

Each menu is coupled with a so-called module, which is administered in the Module Manager (see Section 4.8). The four menus are shown to you in the Menu Manager workspace and in the menu bar (see Figure 4.44).

You can access the existing menus from the menu bar or by clicking the respective menu item icon in the Menu Manager. The editing steps are the same for all menus:

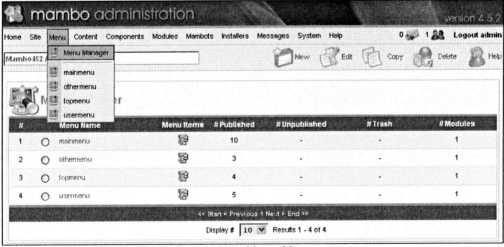

Figure 4.44: Menu Manager

4.5.1 Customize Existing Menu

Go to Site | Menu Manager | mainmenu (Figure 4.45). The first published menu entry on this list is shown as the starting page of your site. At the moment this is the front page. But you can make any other element the starting page:

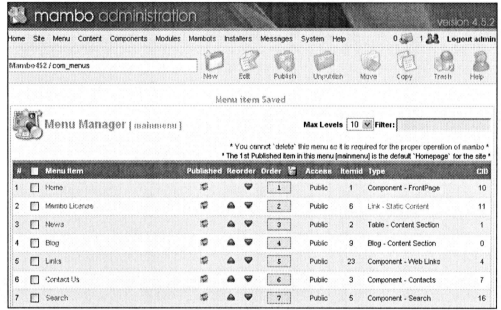

Figure 4.45: MainMenu

New

We will create a new menu in the next section.

Edit

Here you can modify an existing menu, for example, the links. After one click on the name link, you get the form for modification of menu elements as shown in Figure 4.46.

In the left area, you can set up the details and on the right the parameters. The number and the type of parameters depends on the type of the menu entry:

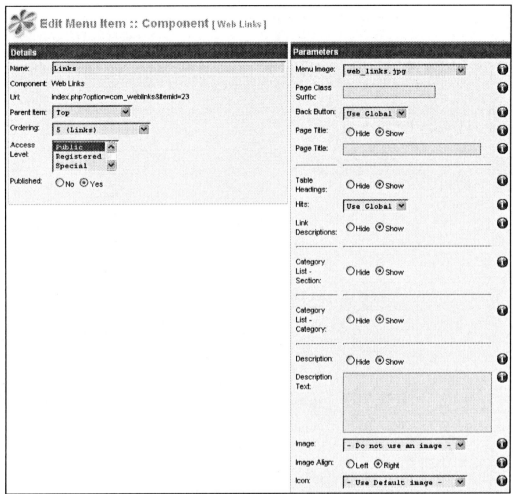

Figure 4.46: Edit Menu

Details

Name: This is the name of the menu that appears on your site.

Component: With this, you find out what type of content is hidden behind the menu entry. This setting is specified while creating the menu entry. In our case, the web links component is being addressed.

Url: This is the call of the components, that is, the part behind the domain with which you access your site. Here, this is index.php?option=com_weblinks&Itemid=23.

Parent Item: The parent item is the superordinate element to this menu. *Top* means at the top level, all other entries represent existing menu entries. If, for example, you arrange and store Links under News, the display in the Menu Manager (Figure 4.47) and the display on your site changes. On the site, the menu entry Links has now slipped into News. You first have to click News, in order to see the Links entry.

This way your site can be structured like a directory tree, very simply and effectively as shown in Figure 4.47:

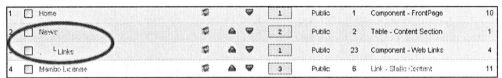

Figure 4.47: Tree Structures in Menu Manager

Ordering: By clicking on the upward and downward pointing triangles you can modify the sort sequence within the menu. In the Ordering field you can do this in a listing. That way you don't have to keep clicking on the triangles.

Figure 4.48: Tree Structures on the Site

Access Level: You can decide whether this menu is to be made available to all visitors (Public), only registered users (Registered), or a special circle of users (Special).

Published: You can publish or lock the menu here.

Parameters
Menu Image: Here you can specify a picture that must be in the root directory of the Media Manager (/images/stories/). Depending on the template, this picture is displayed on the left, next to the menu entry.

Page Class Suffix: Here you can specify a class from the CSS file of your template, with which this menu entry is to be formatted.

Back Button: Here you can assign the global settings for the back button, display it explicitly, or hide it.

Page Title: With this, you can display or hide the title of the page.

Page Title: Here you can specify the page title as shown:

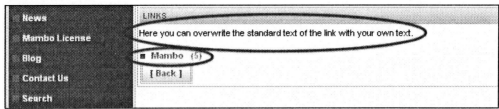

Figure 4.49: Individual Web link Area-1

If you don't enter anything here, the name of the link is assumed.

Table Headings: Here you can display or hide the heading above the listing.

Hits: The hits on the links are displayed in the link list. You can change these in the global settings or via an appropriate selection.

Link Descriptions: Here you can enable the description that is displayed under a link in the link list.

Category List - Section/Category: If you click on Links, you can see the default text or your own text if specified in the parameters. Among them is a list of available categories and sections. This list can be turned on and off with two switches, as shown in Figure 4.49.

Description: Here you can switch the general description of the link components on or off.

Description Text: Here you can overwrite the standard text of the link components with individual text.

Image: Here you can specify a picture, which must be in the root directory of the Media Manager (/images/stories/). Depending on the image align parameter, this picture is displayed on the left or right of the description text, as illustrated in Figure 4.50:

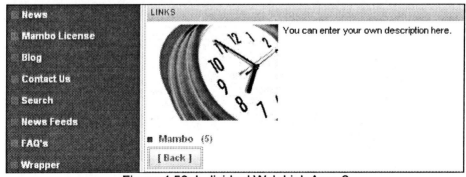

Figure 4.50: Individual Web Link Area-2

Image Align: This is the setting for the adjustment of the picture (see Figure 4.50).

Icon: This is the icon, which is displayed to the left of the list of links.

Publish
If you select one or more menu elements and click the publish icon, they are published.

Unpublish
If you click Unpublish, marked entries are no longer displayed on the site.

Move
This entails moving of menu entries. Select one or several menu elements and click Move. This opens a form, listing the available menus (Figure 4.51). Select the menu into which you would like to move the marked menu entries:

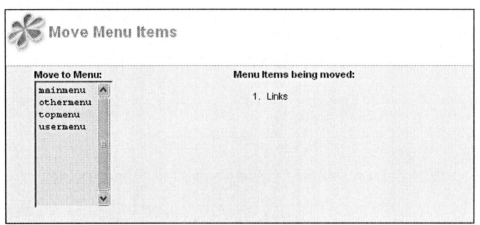

Figure 4.51: Move Menu

Copy
In order to copy menu entries, select one or several menu elements and click Copy. A form is opened, listing the available menus. Select the menu into which you want to copy the marked menu entries.

Trash
In order to throw menu entries into the wastepaper basket, select one or several menu elements and click on the trash icon. The marked menu entries are then dumped into the trash can.

4.5.2 Create a new Menu

Let's create a new menu with the name Mambobook and a link to http://www.google. co.in/. Go to Menu | Menu Manager | New:

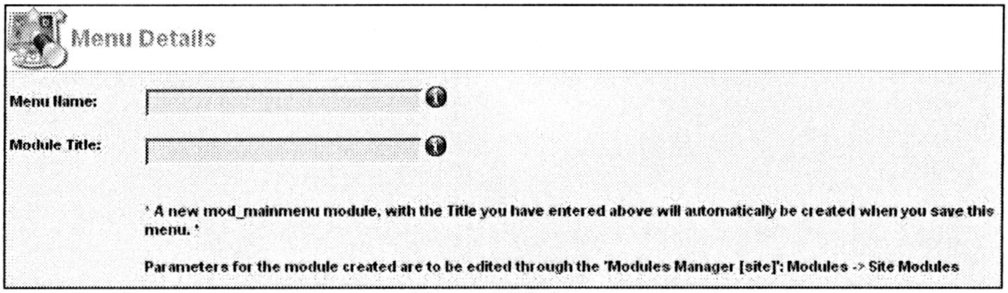

Figure 4.52: New

Menu Name: The name of the menu. This name does not show up on the site, it only serves to make a connection between module and menu.

Module Title: The name of the module. Type the word Search into both fields. After clicking Save, Mambo produces a new module with the given name (Figure 4.53):

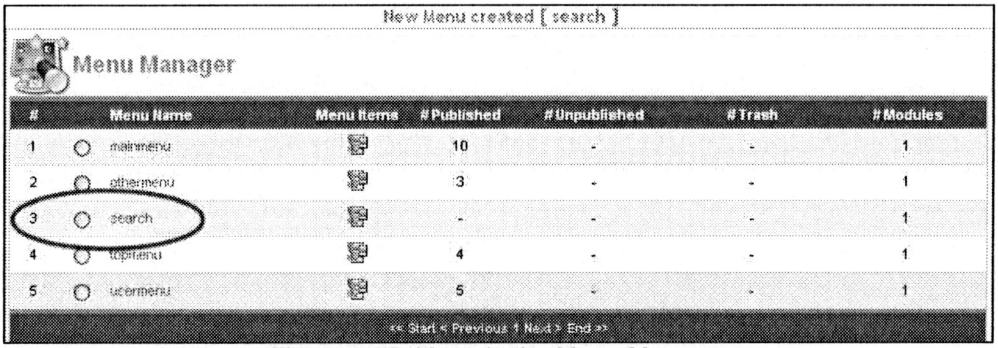

Figure 4.53: Menu in the Menu Manager

Now click the menu items icon or call up Site | Menu Manager | Mambobook in the menu bar. You will see the overview mask about the content of the menu mambobook. Since no content is there yet, click New.

You can now select content from four different areas from the selection mask that appears on your screen (Figure 4.54).

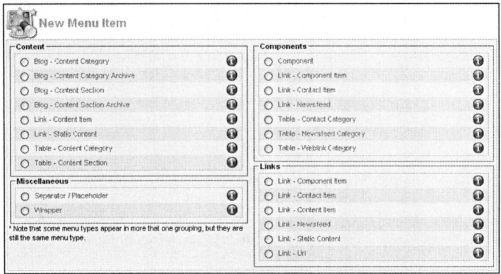

Figure 4.54: New Menu Item

Content

Content is divided into blogs, links, and tables. A blog, in the Mambo sense, is a list of entries with a hook and a read more link. A link refers directly to a certain piece of content. A table is a list of links. A section is a grouping element. Within a section there can be categories. You can find the meaning of the options in table 4.6:

Option	Relevance
Blog – Content Category	Blog page that relates to a category (e.g. latest news).
Blog – Content Category	Archive Blog page that relates to archived categories (no entries as of yet).
Blog – Content Section	Blog page that relates to a section (e.g. news).
Blog – Content Section Archive	Blog page that relates to archived sections (no entries as of yet).
Link – Content Item	Link to a content element (e.g. Sample News Item 2).
Link – Static Content	Direct link to a static content page. There is a static content page in the sample data (*Mambo License Guidelines*).
Table – Content Category	Link to a table that represents the content of a category.
Table – Content Section	Link to a table that represents the content of a section.

Table 4.6: Content Options (Forts)

Miscellaneous:

Option	Relevance
Separator/Placeholder	Insertion of a hyphen into the menu
Wrapper	Here an external page can be displayed within the site; for example, parts of your old site or an already existing guest book.

Table 4.7: Miscellaneous

Components:

Option	Relevance
Link – Component Item	A link to a component (e.g. login)
Link – Contact Item	A link to an entry in the contact list
Link – Newsfeed	A link to a piece of news in the news section
Table – Contact Category	A link to a table that contains entries of a contact category
Table – Newsfeed Category	A link to a table that contains entries of a newsfeed category
Table – Weblink Category	A link to a table that contains entries of a weblink category

Table 4.8: Components

Links:

Option	Relevance
Link – Component Item	A link to a component (e.g. login)
Link – Contact Item	A link to an entry in the contact list
Link – Content Item	A link to a content item (e.g. Sample News Item 2)
Link – Newsfeed	A link to a piece of news from the news section
Link – Static Content	Direct link to a static content page. There is a static content page in the sample data (*Mambo License Guidelines*).

Option	Relevance
Link – Url	Link to a URL (e.g. `http://www.google.co.in/`)

Table 4.9: New Menu Item – Links (Forts)

In order to insert a link to a URL, you mark the last selection field Link – Url and click Next in the toolbar. You can specify the details and the parameters of the link in the form that opens on your screen (Figure 4.55):

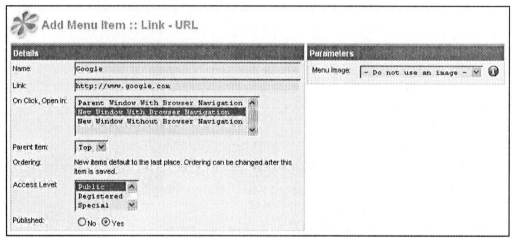

Figure 4.55: Add Menu Item :: Link - URL

Name: Name of the link that appears in the menu (Google)

Link: The link to the page (`http://www.google.com/`)

On Click, Open in: What is to happen, if someone clicks on the link? Should the target be executed in the same browser window, a new browser window with navigation, or a new browser window without navigation?

Parent Item: Should the menu entry be a submenu of a superordinate entry?

Access Level: Should the menu entry be visible to Public (visitors), Registered, or Special groups?

Published: Should the menu be published?

If you click Apply, your data is stored. By clicking on Save, the data is stored and the dialog is closed. Now you have created the menu and provided it with a link. Before it can be displayed, you have to publish the module in the Module Manager. Click Modules | Site Modules (Figure 4.56) and then Published:

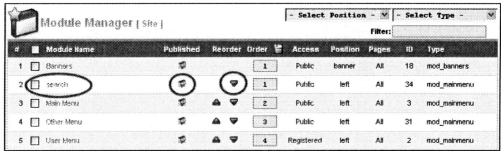
Figure 4.56: Site Modules

You can change the position of the menu with the help of the blue triangles. If you now call up your site, your new Mambobook menu should be displayed above the main menu (Figure 4.57):

Figure 4.57: New Menu Mambobook

By clicking the Google link, a browser window with navigation should open and the Google homepage should be displayed.

4.6 Content Menu

The Content menu contains all content areas. Content is organized by the following structure in Mambo:

Content	-+-	Section1	-+-	Category1	-+-	Content1
	|		|		+-	Content2
	|		|		+-	Content3
	|		+-	Category2	+-	Content1
	|		+-			Content2
	+-	Section1	-+-	Category1	-+-	Content1
	|		|		+-	Content2
	|		|		+-	Content3
	|		+-	Category2	+-	Content1
	|				+-	Content2
	+-	Static Content	-+-	Content1		
			+-	Content2		
			+-	Content3		

Figure 4.58: Content Organized by Mambo

This structure can be compared with the directory tree on your hard drive. You can create as many sections, categories, and as much static content as you desire. If you archive individual elements, then the structure is completely transferred to the archive. The content menu makes different workspaces available, in order to work on content and structures (Figure 4.59):

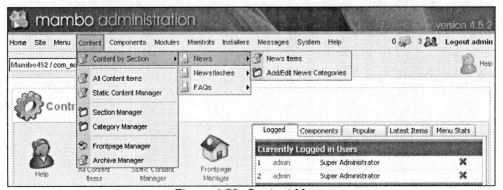

Figure 4.59: Content Menu

4.6.1 Content by Section

Content is sorted according to section. The next step in the structure is Category; the actual content then follows (Items).

Section

Underneath the Content by Section menu, all available sections are shown. You can add as many sections as you want.

Category

Underneath each section you again find a listing of the existing categories, as well as the option to work on these categories.

Add/Edit Section Category

Here you can create a new category, by clicking New. Let us use the category Mambobook as an example.

Category Title: The title of the category that appears in the title line of the browser.

Category Name: The name of the category that will be displayed on the site.

Section: The section in which the category is to be created, in our case, *The News*.

Image: Here you can select a picture that will be displayed when the site is accessed. The picture has to be in the Media Manager root directory (/images/stories/). I have selected .jpg articles.

Image Position: Here you can select the orientation of the picture.

Ordering: Here the order of the category is determined. In this case it is a new element, which by default is integrated at the end. The sequence can be changed after it has been saved once.

Access Level: Who has access to this element?

Published: Should the category be published immediately?

Description: This is the description of the category. If you selected the WYSIWYG editor in Site | Global Configuration | Site (Section 4.4.1), a basic word processor will pop up:

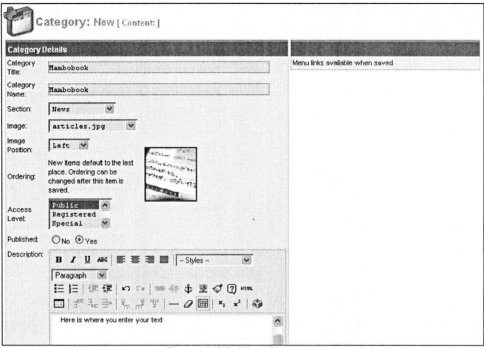

Figure 4.60: New Category

You can only specify parameters for this category after it has been saved once by clicking Save. You wind up in the Category Manager and will see the new category Mambobook (Figure 4.61):

#		Category Name	Published	Order		Access	Section	Category ID	# Active	# Trash
1	☐	Latest News (Latest)	↻	1		Public	News	1	5	0
2	☐	Mambobook (Mambobook)	↻	2		Public	News	13	0	0
3	☐	Newsflash (Newsflash)	↻	0		Public	Newsflashes	3	3	0
4	☐	Example FAQs (Examples)	↻	0		Public	FAQs	7	2	0

Category saved

Category Manager | Content: All | - Select Section - ⌄

<< Start < Previous 1 Next > End >>

Display # 10 ⌄ Results 1 - 4 of 4

Figure 4.61: Category Manager

Content Item: After we have created a new category, we want to insert content into this category. Click Content | Content by Section | News | News Items.

You are now put into the Content Items Manager and can see the four standard entries of the Mambo sample data.

Click New in order to be transferred to the workspace content item:

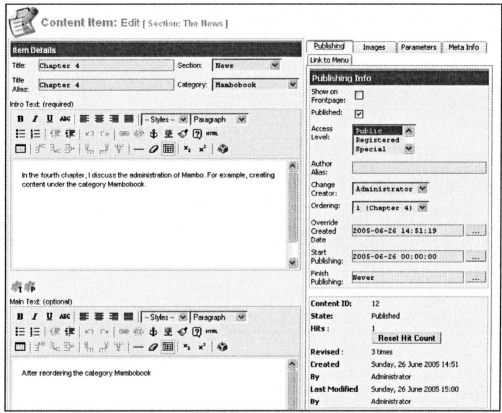

Figure 4.62: Content Item Workspace

You will see a form consisting of several areas. Actual content is located in the left panel; in the right panel are several tabs with different parameters. It is sufficient to fill out the left side at this time in order to write information.

Title: Title of the item of information

Title Alias: Alias of the title

Section: Here you can select a *section* where the message is to be displayed. Select News.

Category: Depending on the section selected, the existing categories are shown.
Select Mambobook.

Intro Text/Main Text: Here you enter your actual information. The intro text has to be filled out, the main text is optional. With one click on Preview, you can see a preview of your text in a separate browser window (Figure 4.63):

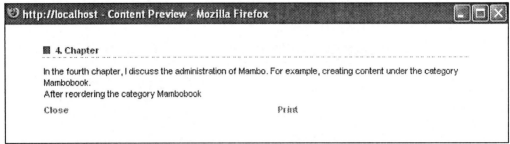

Figure 4.63: Content Preview

In order to integrate the new information immediately into the Search menu, you now click the tab Link to Menu:

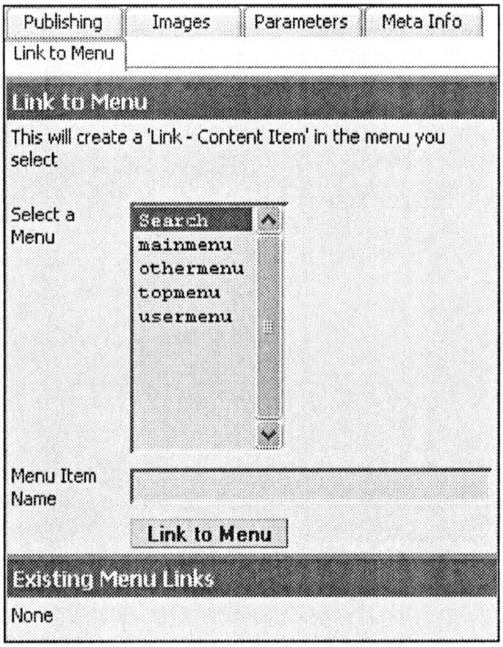

Figure 4.64: Link to Menu

You will see a list of the available menus.

If you select the Search menu, enter Chapter 4 in the Menu Item Name field and click Link to Menu. The page is newly configured and you will see in the lower part of existing menu links that your information has been added to the menu. Click Save.

If you look at your site, you will notice that the search menu has an additional entry.
After a click on the entry you will see your information:

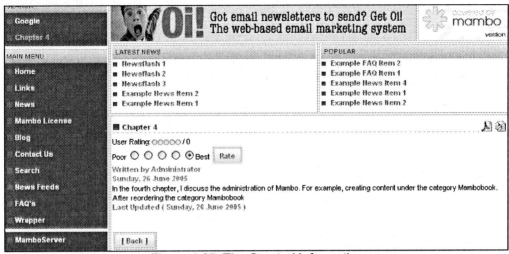

Figure 4.65: The Created Information

4.6.2 All Content Items

The All Content Items menu leads you to the Content Manager:

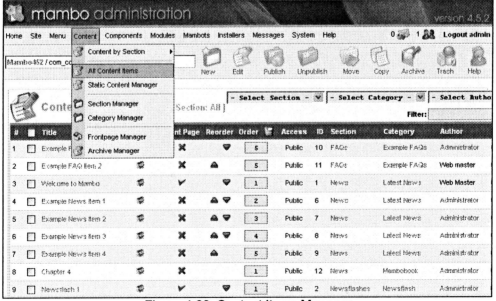

Figure 4.66: Content Items Manager

The Content Manager is the central configuration station for all types of content. You can filter the displayed content by section (area), category, and author in three option lists in the information area. In addition, you will find a search field, with which you can search the titles.

In the lower part is the navigation bar, with whose assistance you can leaf through the contents. In the option list, you can select the number of entries you want to see. The setting that you entered in Site | Global Configuration | Site acts as the default. The list is sorted by section, category, author, and title.

There is a check box in front of the title, with which you can select those elements that you want to work on. If you select the check box in front of the headline, all elements of the list are selected.

The Title is a link to the edit mode for Content Items (Figure 4.62).

Published indicates whether the entry is published (green check mark) or not (red cross). Besides these two symbols, the possibility also exists that the publication period has run out and the element is stored in archives.

Frontpage indicates whether the entry is published on the front page (see Section 4.6.6) (green check mark) or not (red cross).

With Reorder you can move the entries within a section by clicking the blue arrows.

With Order you can execute this sorting by input of a number.

With Access you see green public links. By clicking one of these links you can change the access rights between the three groups: Public, Registered, and Special. In addition there are also symbols for pending (waiting status) and expired (out of date).

ID is the record number in the MySQL table. This ID will show up again in the URL for this entry.

Section is the area to which this entry is assigned. You wind up in the section manager if you click this link.

Category is the category in which this entry is classified. Clicking the link takes you to the Category Manager.

Author is the author of the entry. Click this link and you end up in the User Manager.

Date is the creation date of the entry.

4.6.3 Static Content Manager

The Static Content Manager looks like the Content Manager. However, it does not have any fields for sections and categories.

Static content means something similar to a static HTML page. Normally, content elements and items of information are created and sorted into categories and sections within Mambo. The content elements have a dynamic character, since they are usually displayed in a chronological order:

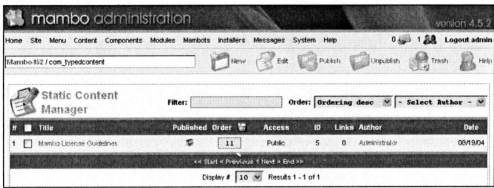

Figure 4.67: Static Content Manager

Static content is fixed and refers to content that rarely changes and that has no chronological connection to other content elements. You can find a sample of static content in the sample data, e.g. the license guidelines for using Mambo (Mambo Licence Guidelines).

Click New and we'll run an example through the Static Content Manager by creating your imprint.

You will see an input mask, just like in Figure 4.68. This time, however, there will be a text field. Enter imprint as *title* or *alias title* and enter your address as text. Click Apply.

Publishing

Parameters that have to do with publishing are defined with this.

State: Current status (currently published).

Published: Check box to change the status.

Access Level: Access rights for the three user groups.

Author Alias: Here you can enter a pseudonym for the author.

Change Creator: Here you can change the creator of the information.

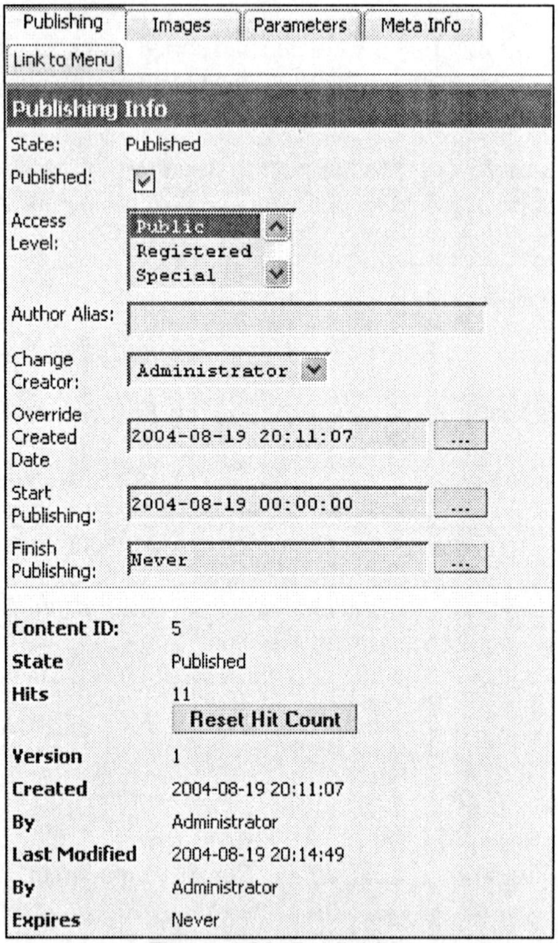

Figure 4.68: Publishing

Override Created Date: At this point you can change the creation date of the item. Clicking on the three dots will get the graphic calendar to help you with the input of dates, as shown in Figure 4.69.

Start Publishing: This serves to specify the start date of the publication. By default, content is published immediately. By clicking the three dots, a graphic calendar is displayed for input assistance (as shown in Figure 4.69).

Finish Publishing: Here you can determine the expiration date of the content. The default is that content is *never* purged. Click the three dots to call up the graphic calendar again (as shown in Figure 4.69):

Figure 4.69: Calendar Element

Content ID: The record number

Hits: How often the content has been accessed.

Version: The document has the version number 1. Each time it is saved, the version number is increased by one.

Images

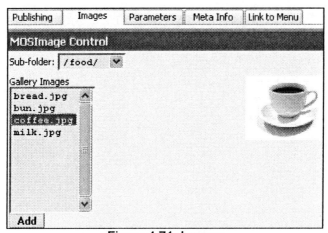

Figure 4.71: Images

You can assign any picture from the Media Manager to any piece of content. If it is available yet in the Media Manager, you can upload it while working on the content by clicking Upload:

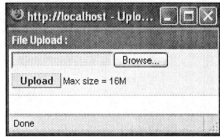

Figure 4.70: Upload

You cannot, however, indicate a target subdirectory for this type of file upload. Select a subdirectory and click on a picture as shown. You will see a preview of the picture on the right side and now you just have to click Add. In the window below it, you can now see the filename:

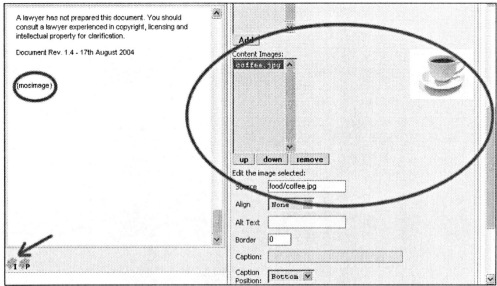

Figure 4.72: Mapping a Picture into the Text

If you click on it, the picture preview appears. You can assign as many image files as you wish. You still have to specify the position in the text, where the picture is to be displayed. To do that, you need a Mambot with the name {mosimage}.

Refer to Section 4.9 for more information about Mambots. Position the cursor at the position where the picture is to appear. Either type {mosimage} manually or click the Mambo logo with the I under the text window. You have to insert one Mambot for every picture that you want to insert. Beside the I-logo there is also a P-logo.

This is a Mambot that represents a page break {mospagebreak}. If you have text that you want to distribute over several pages, you have to insert this Mambot.

For the display on the site, Mambo automatically produces a navigation bar to help you scroll through the content:

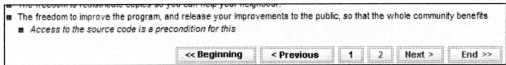

Figure 4.73: Navigation Bar

Parameters

In the Parameter tab you can overwrite the parameters that were defined in Site | Global Configuration for this content:

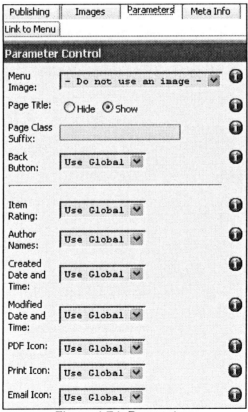

Figure 4.74: Parameters

Meta Info

In this tab you can enter a specific description and keywords for every page as metadata. The text entered here is then inserted into the HTML metatags:

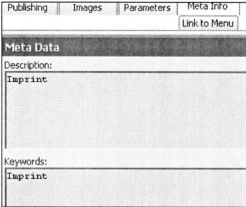

Figure 4.75: Meta Info

Link to Menu

Automatic links to a menu, for example, the main menu, can be created here (see Section 4.6.3). The site displays multipaged content (Figure 4.76 and Figure 4.77):

Figure 4.76: Imprint – Page 1

The evaluation and other parameters can also be faded individually.

Figure 4.77: Imprint – Page 2

4.6.4 Section Manager

In Section Manager you can work on the sections. In the overview table, the information that you already know from the other lists is displayed, but in this case it is expanded to the number of total categories contained—how many are active and how many are in the trash can (Figure 4.78):

#		Section Name	Published	Reorder	Order	Access	Section ID	#Categories	#Active	#Trash
1	☐	The News (News)	✓	▼	1	Public	1	2	6	0
2	☐	Frequently Asked Questions (FAQs)	✓	▲ ▼	2	Public	3	1	2	0
3	☐	Newsflashes (Newsflashes)	✓	▲	2	Public	2	1	3	0

<< Start < Previous 1 Next > End >>

Display # 10 ▾ Results 1 - 3 of 3

Figure 4.78: Section Manager

4.6.5 Category Manager

In the Category Manager you can work on categories. Here you will also see familiar information in the overview table: how many of the categories are active, and how many are in the trash can (Figure 4.79):

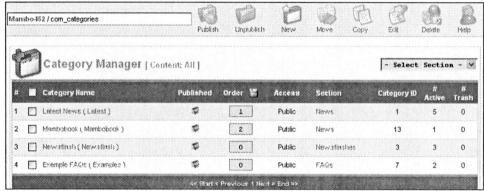

Figure 4.79: Category Manager

4.6.6 Frontpage Manager

The Frontpage Manager has a special task. The frontpage is the title page of your website. Selected content is here represented in blog form. Blog form means the representation of several pieces of information with its introduction text and a Read More link in several columns. You can select your content for the frontpage from all of the content, regardless of category and section. Whether content appears on the frontpage is specified by you in the Content Manager.

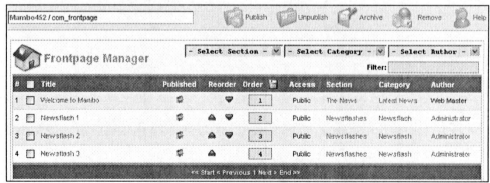

Figure 4.80: Frontpage Manager

The Frontpage Manager as illustrated above has the same structure as the Content Items Manager (Figure 4.66). You can also sort the individual content items within the Frontpage Manager.

4.6.7 Archive Manager

The idea of archives is to not delete outdated content, but to preserve it for posterity:

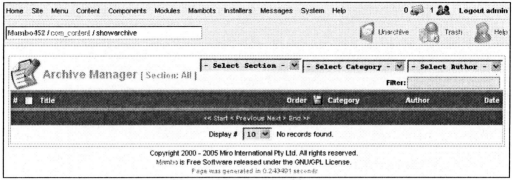

Figure 4.81: Archive Manager

Laid out like the Content Items Manager (Figure 4.66), the Archive Manager (Figure 4.81) collects all content that is archived by clicking the archive icon.

Archives can be displayed by the Menu Manager in, for example, a new archives menu. In addition, there are the following possibilities, as has been illustrated in Figure 4.54:

Blog – Content Category Archive: Display of a particular archive category

Blog – Content Section Archive: Display of a section

4.7 Components Menu

In software development, a component or a Java Bean means a program that contains business logic, is accessible through defined interfaces, and sometimes also has a user interface. Imagine a simple component acting like a so-called black box: I put something in the front and something comes out the back: I don't have to know what happens inside. What matters is that I can use the black box for completely different purposes.

Components can be designed very generally and bundled into handy packages. This idea of a software component is similar in Mambo. Business logic, such as banner administration or a forum, is written generally and in Mambo works in concert with all the templates and Mambo administration.

4.7.1 Install/Uninstall

Anyone can write a component, package it according to certain rules, and install it as per Mambo installation into his or her Mambo system:

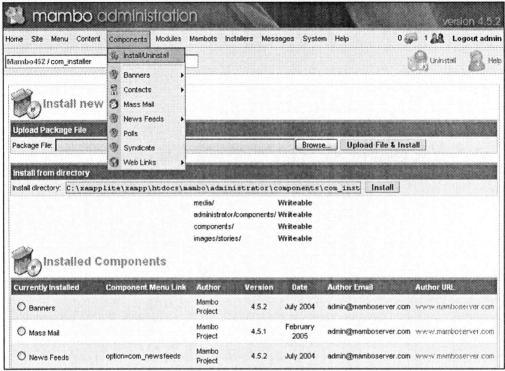

Figure 4.82: Install/Uninstall

The installation, as with the language files, is executed either by file or FTP upload of the component package.

The necessary database tables are created during the installation. The installation fields indicate whether the necessary directories for the installation, media/administrator/components/, components/, and images/stories/ are provided with write rights.

Installed Components
In the Installed Components workspace, you can see a list of components installed by default.

Currently Installed: Name of the components.

Component Menu Link: Necessary parameter in the URL, in order to access the component. Only components addressable from the homepage need this link.

Author: The author of the component.

Version: The component version.

Date: The creation date.

Author E-Mail: E-mail of the author.

Author Url: Homepage of the author.

4.7.2 Banner

The banner component makes the display of advertising banners on your site possible. Banner switching with Mambo is accounted for, on the basis of bought banner impressions. Each time your site is accessed, another banner is displayed. Every display counts as an impression. The banner is clickable and links to the site of the customer.

The banner component offers customer and banner administration. By default, the so-called full banner is sent. A full banner is 468 x 60 pixels large and should not substantially exceed 20 KB in file size. The format is `.gif`, `.jpg`, or `.png`.

Let's walk through a banner switch. Create or copy a banner with the dimensions of 468 x 60 pixels as shown:

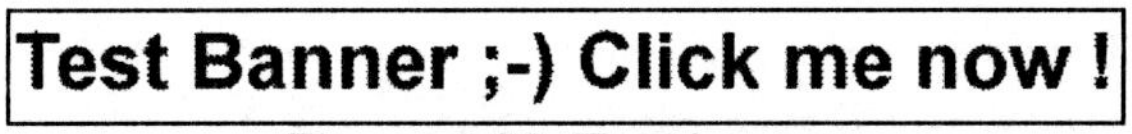

Test Banner ;-) Click me now !
Figure 4.83: Test banner

Manage Clients

Before you can switch a banner, you need a customer. If you click Components | Banner | Manage Clients | New, you are opening a new customer account. Store it by clicking Save.

The Banner Client Manager, where you wind up, now displays your new customer as well as the number of active banners of this customer:

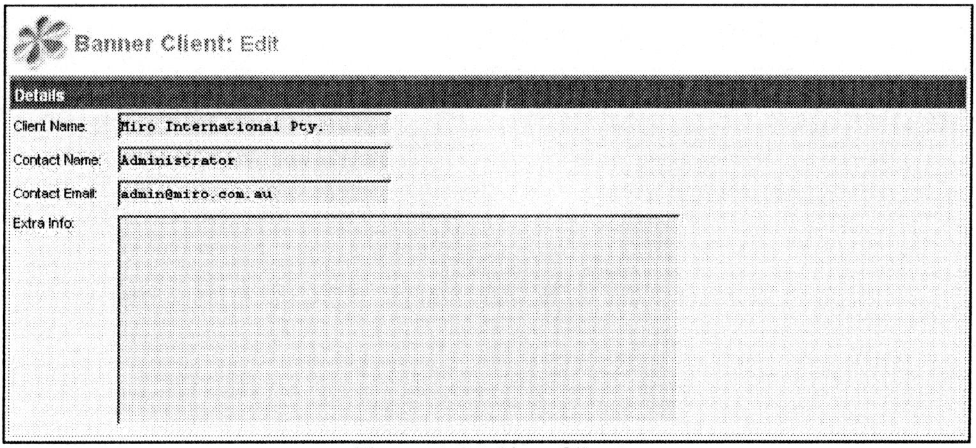

Figure 4.84: New Client

Manage Banners

In order to be able to assign a banner to the customer, click on Components | Banners | Manage Banners. You can see the Banner Manager, which gives you an overview of the existing banners as shown:

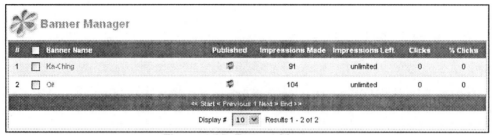

Figure 4.85: Banner Manager

Banner Name: Name of the banner

Published: Whether the banner is published or not

Impressions Made: Number of impressions to date

Impressions Left: Number of remaining impressions

Clicks: Clicks on the banner

% Clicks: Proportion of impressions to clicks

In order to switch to a new banner, you first click on the upload icon. A small upload window opens for uploading banners. The banners don't emerge in the Media Manager, but are stored in the directory /image/banner/. If you want to delete a banner again, that can only be done currently by a FTP client. After you have uploaded the banner, click New and fill out the banner as shown in Figure 4.86:

Banner Name: Give the banner a meaningful name so that you will recognize it in the Banner Manager.

Client Name: Select the client from the list of current clients.

Impressions Purchased: Enter the number of purchased impressions or check the Unlimited box.

Banner URL: Select the just-uploaded banner from the list of the existing banners. After the selection, you will see a preview of the banner in the lower area.

Show Banner: Should the banner be published?

Click URL: Enter the URL of the site to which the banner is supposed to be linking.

Custom banner code: Here you can enter a special banner code from affiliate programs.

Since this mask is also designed for the editing of banners, you will find the indicator of the clicks already executed and a reset button, which sets it back to zero.

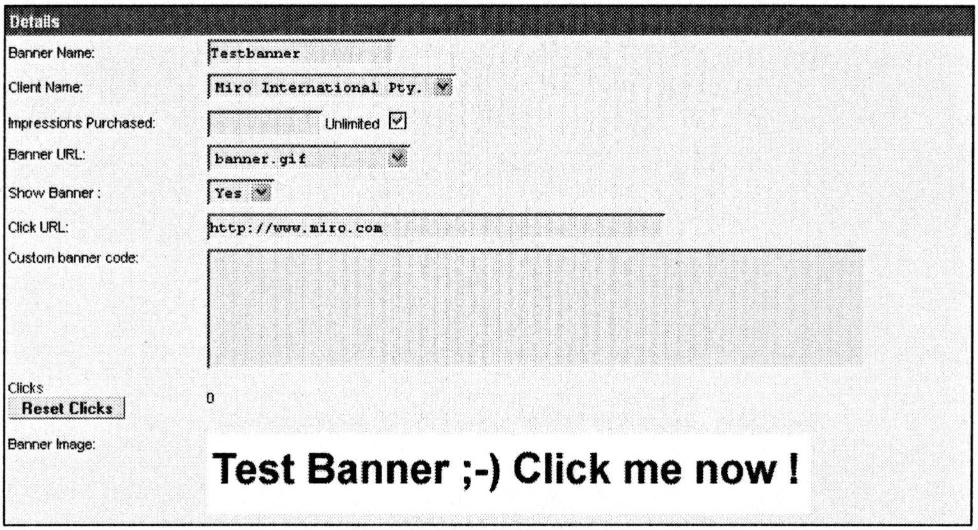

Figure 4.86: New Banner

After clicking the save icon, your banner should be in rotation and displayed on the site:

Figure 4.87: Client Banner on the Homepage

4.7.3 Contacts

It is often difficult for a customer surfing your site to contact you. Many employees normally work in different departments in companies and often only one address (for example, info@company.com) is shown on the homepage or on a form and the customer has no idea who receives it.

To avoid this, Mambo makes it possible to specify contact categories. You can register contact persons for your company. Mambo then produces a contact form for every coworker on the site.

Manage Contacts

Click Components | Contacts | Manage Contacts. You will see the Contact Manager and a contact from the sample data as shown:

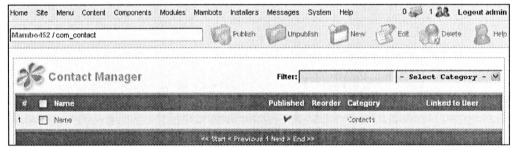

Figure 4.88: Contact Manager

Mark the sample contact and click Unpublish. You can create a new contact with New as shown in Figure 4.89.

Category: Select the contact category here. At the moment, the sample category Contacts is available.

Linked to User: With this option you can connect a contact with a user account. Since I have already created an account for myself, I can now select it.

You can populate the remaining fields with the appropriate address data and add some text as miscellaneous information. In order to store it, click on the save icon:

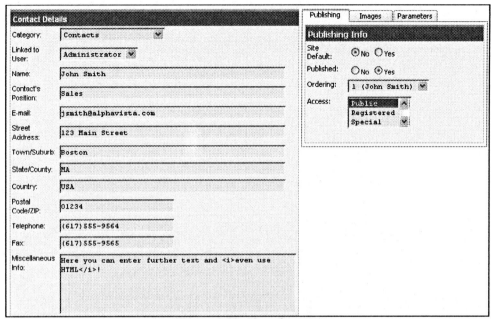

Figure 4.89: New Contact

Since we did not publish the sample entry, there is currently only one contact in the system. There is no necessity to show categories. Because of this, the contact link branches immediately to that one entry. If you publish the sample entry again, the following window pops up:

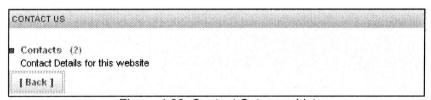

Figure 4.90: Contact Category List

The existing contact categories are displayed here. After clicking on the category, you get a table with the existing contacts:

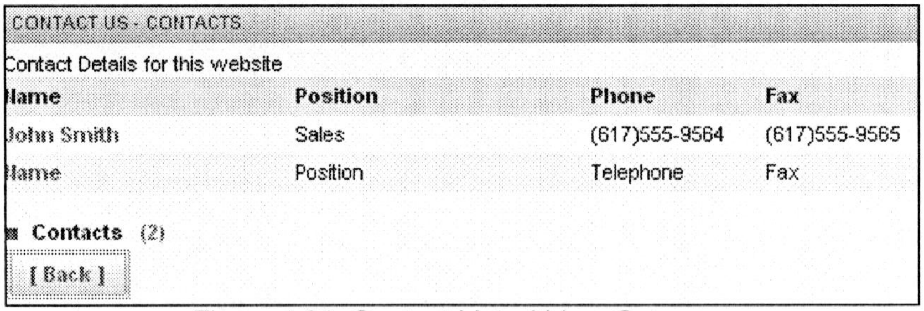

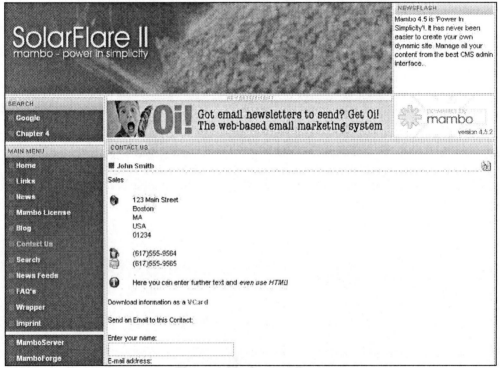

Figure 4.91: Contact List within a Category

If you now click on the name, you get the contact form:

Figure 4.92: Contact Form

I'm sure you noticed the tabs when you created the contact. In the Publishing tab (as illustrated in Figure 4.93) you can specify the default contact (Site Default).

In addition, you can specify the publication, ordering, and access rights:

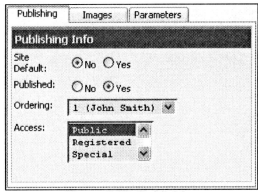
Figure 4.93: Publishing

Under Images, as shown in Figure 4.94 you can assign a picture to each contact. Photograph your staff and let your customers know what the guy they are writing to looks like:

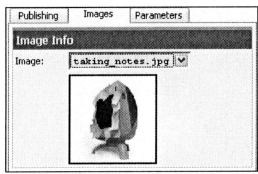
Figure 4.94: Images

Under Parameters, the contact form can finally be completely individualized. You can even change the icons next to the telephone numbers. The available icons are in the subdirectory /images/M_images/and cannot be accessed via the Media Manager.

Contacts Categories
In the Category Manager for contacts, you can create new categories and modify existing ones:

Figure 4.95: Category Manager

An editing form pops up after clicking the edit icon or the category name:

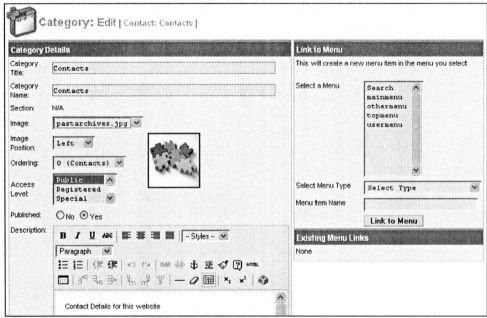

Figure 4.96 Edit

You can assign a picture here and you can make changes to the description with the help of the WYSIWYG editor. In the space on the right, the category can immediately be assigned to a particular menu. You can also decide whether you want to have the table listing or a listing of all categories first (Select Menu Type).

4.7.4 Mass Mail

Delight your users with mass mail! As cynical as this sentence sounds, in the age of massive spam e-mailing, mass mailing is the best way of contacting one's registered users. The Mass Mail component gives you the tool to do it.

Group: Here you can select the user group that the mass mailing is to be addressed to.

Mail to Child Groups: If you put a checkmark here, the subgroups of the selected user groups are also addressed.

Send in HTML mode: Check this if you want to send the mass mail in HTML format. HTML mail is becoming more and more popular. You should, however, keep in mind that many e-mail clients can switch the HTML display off. For different reasons, some users may not even like HTML mail.

Subject: This is the subject of your e-mail.

Message: This is the actual text.

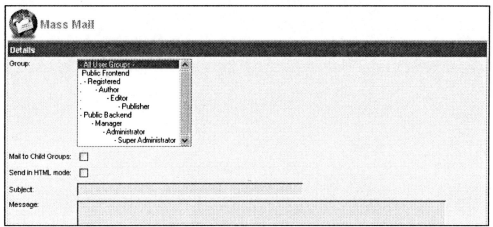

Figure 4.97: Mass Mail

For mass mailing, set the mail settings in Site | Global Configuration | Mail correctly. If you want to send a mass mail from your local environment, but are not running a mail server, then you can also register the SMTP server of your mail provider in the mass mail settings.

4.7.5 News Feeds

News feeds are a terrific thing. The ever-growing information abundance on the Internet makes it necessary to test effective organizational methods. If you regularly have to visit twenty web pages to check what's new, it takes up too much time. With fifty or hundred it is absolutely hopeless to try to keep an overview. News feeds are an attempt to solve this problem. What they are and how they are produced is covered in Section 4.7.7.

With the news feed component you can merge feeds from other pages into your pages. To do that, a Category Manager and a Content Manager are at your disposal. The sample data already has several categories and numerous news feeds incorporated. Integrate your own news feed. You can use a search engine for this purpose or look for the small XML button at the sites that you visit.

Manage Newsfeeds

A click on Components | News Feeds | Manage New Feeds | New allows you to fill in your preferences:

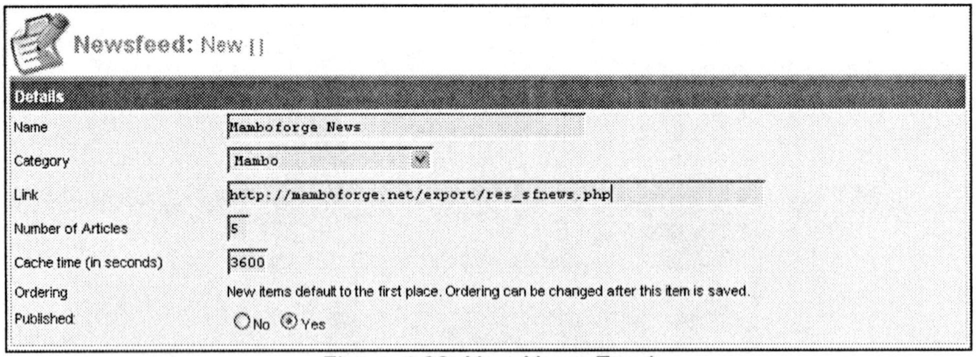

Figure 4.98: New News Feed

Name: This is the name of the news feed that appears on your page.

Category: Select a suitable category from the existing ones.

Link: This is the link to the news feed.

Number of Articles: This refers to the number of articles that are to be merged.

Cache time (in seconds): How long should the break between the actualizations be (in seconds)?

Ordering: This is the sequence new news feeds will start at, by default. The sequence can be changed after it has been saved once.

Published: Should it be published immediately?

Your new news feed, as long as you have Internet access, is displayed on your site:

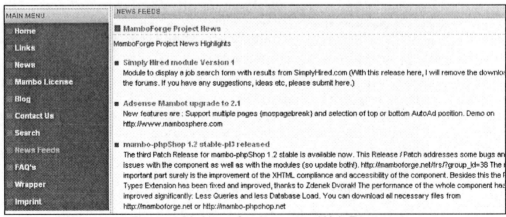

Figure 4.99: News feeds on your Web Page

Since there are differences between the character sets of individual languages, there may be problems in the display of special characters and HTML commands. This is dependent on many factors. It depends, for example, on whether the special characters were produced with Unicode or with a regional character set. By the way, the operator of the news feed should not insert HTML commands. On the other hand, the Mambo function should also be improved when it comes to the presentation. Just try it out. The result is not exactly predictable.

Manage Categories

Here you can administer the news feed categories. The administration functions are similar to the Contacts Category Manager shown in Figure 4.95.

4.7.6 Polls

The integrated poll module makes it possible for you to publish polls on your site. One poll is already included in the sample data as illustrated below:

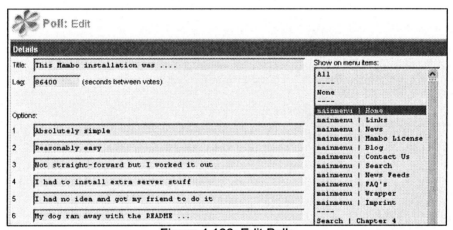

Figure 4.100: Edit Polls

Title: This is the title of your poll.

Lag: This determines the time in seconds that has to elapse before another selection can be made. This lag offers some kind of protection from the falsification of survey data.

Options: Here you can enter up to twelve answer options.

Show on menu items: You can select in which area of the site the poll is to be displayed. Multiple options are possible by holding down the *Control* key and clicking the left mouse button.

Click Preview to get a preview of your poll. To display it on your site, make sure that polls are provided in the current template. Now see the poll on your site:

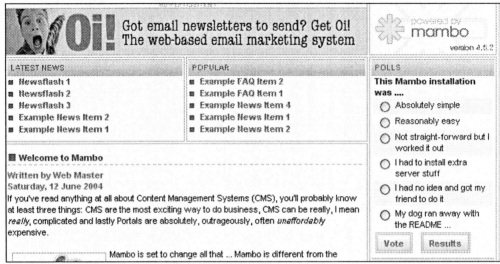
Figure 4.101: Poll on the Site

If you try the poll out and select an answer, an analysis appears:

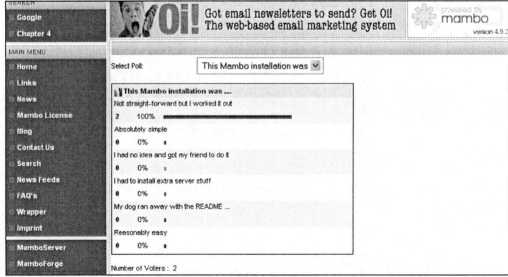
Figure 4.102: Poll Analysis on the Site

The poll itself is no longer displayed, since by default it was attached only to the front page. Attaching the poll to the individual pages can be configured in the Module Manager (see Section 4.8.2).

4.7.7 Syndicates

In the syndicate component, parameters for producing news feeds can be specified.

A news feed is an XML file that adheres to current standards (Listing 4.1). You can create this file by clicking the RSS 0.91 option on your site, as illustrated:

Figure 4.103: Syndication of
News Feeds

This file is not intended to be read, but serves as an exchange format between two programs.

Normally one doesn't transfer the file, but only hands over the appropriate URL:

`http://localhost/mambo/index2.php?option=com_rss&feed=RSS0.91&no_html=1`

The file creation and the visual preparation are handled by the reading program.

Listing 4.1: XML-News Feed in RSS 0.91Format created by Mambo

```
<?xml version="1.0" encoding="ISO-8859-1" ?>
<!-- generator="FeedCreator 1.7.2" -->
<rss version="0.91">
<channel>
<title>Powered by Mambo 4.5.2</title>
<description>Mambo site syndication</description>
<link>http://localhost/mambo</link>
<lastBuildDate>Mon,14 Mar 2005 13:38:08</lastBuildDate>
<generator>FeedCreator 1.7.2</generator>
<image>
<url>http://localhost/mambo/images/M_images/mambo_rss.png</url>
<title>Powered by Mambo 4.5.2</title>
<link>http://localhost/mambo</link>
<description>Mambo site syndication</description>
</image>
<item>
<title>Welcome to Mambo</title>
<link>http://localhost/mambo/index.php?option=com_content&task=view&i
d=1&Itemid=9</link>
<description>If you've read anything at all about Content Management
Systems (CMS), you'll probably know at least three things: CMS are
the...</description>
</item>
```

```
<item> ... </item>
... additional items
</channel>
</rss>
```

The title and text of the latest news messages are located in the file, as well as other information; for example, the time of production, from which site the messages come from and direct links to the pages.

Mambo can create news feeds and support the following standards:

- RSS 0.91/1.0/2.0
- ATOM 0.3
- OPML
- SHARE IT

The content of the feeds can be influenced as follows:

Cache: Should the feeds be cached, to avoid them being recreated for every request?

Cache Time: Here you can specify how long the data should be cached (in seconds).

Items: How many entries should be transferred to the feed?

Title: What is the title of your feed?

Description: What should the description of your feed be?

Image: What picture link should be assigned to the feed? It might make sense to use the logo of your company.

Image Alt: What should be displayed if the receiving terminal cannot read pictures?

Limit Text: Should the text to be transferred be limited to a certain length?

Text Length: How long should the text be?

Order: How should the news be ordered?

- The same as on the front page (*Frontpage Ordering*)
- The *oldest first*
- The most *recent first*
- Alphabetically by title (*Title Alphabetical*)
- Reverse alphabetically by title (*Title Reverse-Alphabetical*)
- Alphabetically by author (*Author Alphabetical*)
- Reverse alphabetically by author (*Author Reverse-Alphabetical*)

- By *most* hits
- By *least* hits

Live Bookmarks: Live bookmarks are a function of the Mozilla Firefox browser. These are dynamic bookmarks that display information from feeds instead of static text. If you are working with Firefox, select RSS 2.00 from the list, and store the parameters.

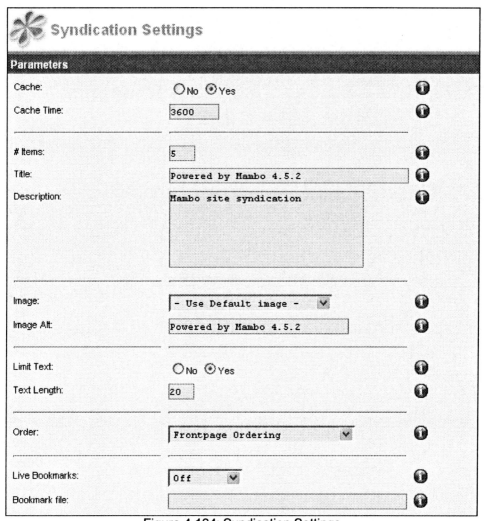

Figure 4.104: Syndication Settings

If you visit your homepage with Firefox, you will see a bright orange XML display in the right lower corner of the browser with the news feed from your site. Here you can view your news messages by clicking this item as shown:

Figure 4.105: Live Bookmark Offer with the Firefox Browser

If you look in your bookmarks later, you will still see the headings of your messages:

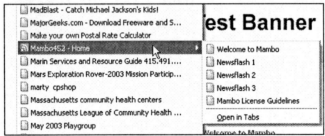

Figure 4.106: Live Bookmarks in Firefox

4.7.8 Weblinks

Here you create a link list that you can integrate into your site. Mambo offers categories and counts the hits on the links. In the user menu, you can let your registered users suggest links that should be included in this list. These suggested links wind up in the weblinks items list and still have to be published.

Weblink Items

You can enter individual links here as shown:

Name: Name of the link that is displayed on the site.

Category: Selection of an available link category.

URL: The URL of the link.

Description: Here you can enter a detailed description of the link.

Ordering: Ordering of links

Approved: Has this link been approved?

Published: Should the link be published?

Target: In the parameter area, you can select whether the link should be displayed in a new window (with or without navigation) or whether it should be displayed in the same window.

120

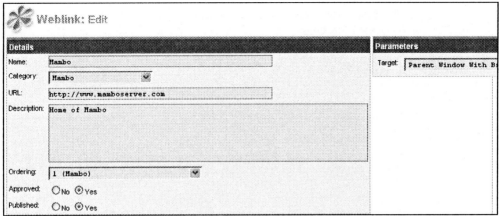

Figure 4.107: Edit Weblinks

Weblink Categories

The link categories are administrated in the respective **Category Manager**:

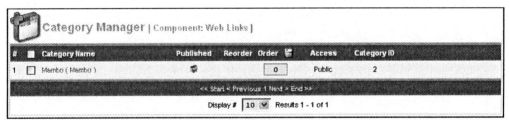

Figure 4.108: Categories

4.8 Module Menu

A module is simpler than a component. It is a code fragment or a snippet that is inserted and interpreted by another part of the program.

Because of the capabilities of the PHP script language, modules can collect data from all kinds of sources. This could be a source on your own site—say, the last five articles, or the weather, foreign exchange rate, Amazon, or an e-bay web service.

A module contains business logic and a user interface. Unlike most components, it does not have its own administration area. The template of your site calls and starts the different modules directly.

Since the modules are independent programs, they can perform something particular in this area of the template, for example, display a banner. A template doesn't do anything, but groups many different modules in a visually appealing way. The module structure has an advantage because you can easily expand your site.

Since you can use templates for your site and for Mambo administration, there are also various modules for these templates.

4.8.1 Install/Uninstall

Here you can install file packages for modules by file upload or from a directory:

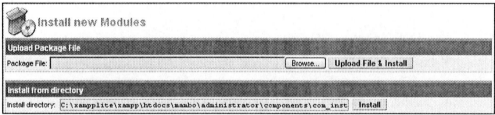

Figure 4.109: Install/Uninstall Modules

For uninstalling, select the module and click Delete. Below the installation area, you can see a list of the installed modules with the origin of the modules and other information.

4.8.2 Site Modules

The Module Manager is the central place for the administration of modules:

#		Module Name	Published	Reorder	Order	Access	Position	Pages	ID	Type
1		Banners	✓		1	Public	banner	All	18	mod_banners
2		search	✓	▼	1	Public	left	All	34	mod_mainmenu
3		Main Menu	✓	▲ ▼	2	Public	left	All	3	mod_mainmenu
4		Other Menu	✓	▲ ▼	3	Public	left	All	31	mod_mainmenu
5		User Menu	✓	▲ ▼	4	Registered	left	All	2	mod_mainmenu
6		Login Form	✓	▲ ▼	5	Public	left	Varies	4	mod_login
7		Statistics	✗	▲ ▼	6	Public	left	None	7	mod_stats
8		Syndicate	✓	▲ ▼	7	Public	left	Varies	5	mod_rssfeed
9		Template Chooser	✗	▲ ▼	8	Public	left	Varies	10	mod_templatechooser
10		Archive	✗	▲	9	Public	left	None	11	mod_archive

Figure 4.110: Site Modules

Module Name: This is the name of the module and heading on the site.

Published: Is the module published?

Reorder: Here, with help of the blue arrows, you can change the order. With this you can determine, for example, whether the search menu should be displayed above or below the main menu.

Order: Direct ordering, by specifying the position and a single click on the icon next to Order can spare you excessive clicking of the blue arrows.

Access: This refers to the access rights for this module (Public, Registered, and Special).

Position: The position is a specification for the template, where the display of this module is intended. There are eight positions within a template.

- Banner (advertising area)
- Left (left page)
- Right (right side)
- Top
- user1 (user defined 1)
- user2 (user defined 2)
- user3 (user defined 3)
- user4 (user defined 4)

After these positions, you can filter the message for a better overview with the help of the list in the upper area.

Pages: Is the module shown on all or only designated pages?

ID: The record number from the database

Type: There are different types of modules. The type mod_mainmenu, for example, appears several times, since every menu belongs to this type. The individual menus differ only in the parameters.

In order to have a better overview, you can filter the information by these types with the help of the option list within the upper area.

In addition, there is still another filter field with which you can filter the information by search words. These filter mechanisms are quite meaningful and Mambo comes packaged with 21 of these modules as standard.

These modules, to a large extent, function uniformly. Besides the input for name, you also have to decide on which pages your module is displayed and what position the module takes up in the template. The parameter list is particularly important with modules; therefore I will particularly emphasize parameters during further demonstration of the modules.

Banner

This module controls the display of banners. You can use the record member-ID of the customer (banner client) as a parameter and thereby make sure that only banners of this customer are displayed. In addition, you can assign a CSS class to this name. In this case, it would have to be an addition to the class `table`, for example, `table.moduletable`. This enables an individual organization of the module (module class suffix).

Template Chooser

This module allows the visitor to the page to select from various templates. By default, it is deactivated and assigned to the site:

Figure 4.111: Template
Chooser Module

The parameters for this module are:

Max. Name Length: This is the length of the template name in characters, which is shown in the option list. If the name is longer, three dots are attached.

Show Preview: Should the template preview be switched on or off?

Width/Height: This is the width and height of the preview picture in pixels.

Module Class Suffix: Specify the name of a CSS class here. It has to be an addition to the class `table`, for example, `table.moduletable`. Thus you can configure the module individually.

All Menus (mod_mainmenu)

The module `mod_mainmenu` is used for all menus. There are vertical (*main menu*) and horizontal menus (*top menu*). With vertical menus, the option of a *flatlist* is offered. A *flatlist* is simply an enumeration of individual points.

Menu Class Suffix: Here you can enter a special CSS class for the visual organization of the menu.

Module Class Suffix: Here you specify a special CSS class for the visual organization of the module (menu content).

Menu Name: This is the name of the menu.

Menu Style: Should it be vertical, horizontal, or flatlist?

Enable Cache: Should the content of the menu be cached in order to reduce load time?

Show Menu Icons: Should menu icons be displayed? The format of the icons depends on the respective active template.

Menu Icon Alignment: Should the menu icons be positioned in the left or right?

Expand Menu: Should the menu entry always be expanded, even if one clicks on another entry? This function is only meaningful with interlocked menu structures:

Figure 4.112: Menu Nesting

Indent Image: Which icon is to be represented with the sub-structures of a menu entry? You may take the icons from the template, use the Mambo default values, provide each hierarchical level with its own picture, or not use any icons.

Indent Image 1-6: You can define icons for six hierarchical levels here.

Spacer: With horizontal menus, a separator (which you determine here), should be placed between menu entries.

End Spacer: With horizontal menus an end-character can be shown at the end of menu entries. If you want that, specify it here.

Login Form

The login module makes two different views available. If one is not yet logged in, one gets a login form:

Depending on the settings in Site | Global Configuration | Site, it's possible to register again:

Figure 4.113: Login Module

After successful authentication, the display changes to the logout option:

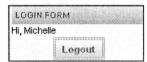

Figure 4.114: Logout Module

The parameters of the Login Form include:

Module Class Suffix: Here you can enter a special CSS class for the visual organization of the menu.

Pre-text: Text that you enter here appears before the form in the login mode.

Post-text: Text that you enter here appears at the end of the module in the login mode.

Login Redirection URL: Here you can determine the URL to which the user is forwarded after a successful login.

Logout Redirection URL: Here you specify the URL to which the user is sent after a successful logout.

Login Message: Should a message in a JavaScript box be displayed after a successful login?

Logout Message: Should a message in a JavaScript box be displayed after a successful logout?

Greeting: After login, the module changes its appearance and displays a greeting text and a logout button. Here can you decide whether you want this text to read: ("hello, username").

Name/Username: Here you determine whether the user is addressed with his/her real name or with his/her username in the greeting text.

Syndicate

In the syndicate module, different news feeds are offered as shown in Figure 4.103.

You can specify in the parameters which standards you are offering and whether you want to use standard pictures or individual pictures. The content of the news feeds offered is given by the entries on the front page.

Statistics

The statistics module is deactivated by default. If you activate it, you must still select the pages on which the statistics are to be displayed. The module supplies information about your server and its site:

Figure 4.115: Statistics Module

The parameters of the Statistics module are:

Server Info: Should the server information be displayed or not?

Site Info: Should the site information be displayed or not?

Hit Counter: Should the visitor counter be integrated or not?

Increase Counter: Here you can specify the initial value of the visitor counter.

Archive

The Archive module, by default, is deactivated. If you activate it, you must select the pages on which it is to be displayed.

It supplies information about the contents of your archive (Figure 4.116). The display is grouped by month:

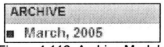

Figure 4.116: Archive Module

The parameters for this module are:

Count: Here you specify the number of displayed months.

Sections

The Sections module is deactivated by default. If you activate it, you must select the pages on which it is to be displayed. It lists the existing sections (Figure 4.117):

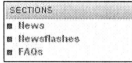

Figure 4.117: Sections
Module

Related Items

The Related Items module indicates other content that is related to this content.

The relationship is based on the keywords specified in the metadata. All keywords of recently displayed content are compared with those of other published content.

If, for example, you register the keyword "law" in the Mambo License Guidelines in the static pages and also in your created imprint, the license guidelines are shown as a related item when you request the imprint:

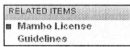

Figure 4.118: Related
Item Module

Wrapper

The Wrapper module wraps external content that is not produced by Mambo, within a so-called iframe. An iframe is an HTML tag and represents a scrollable area within a web page (Figure 4.119):

Figure 4.119: Wrapper-
bound page

With the help of this module you can integrate complete pre-existing HTML pages from other servers into the content area of Mambo.

The parameters for this module are:

URL: Here you can specify a standard URL. The specification of the page that is to be shown, however, usually takes place in the menu allocation (Figure 4.55).

Scroll Bars: Should scrollbars be shown in the iframe? You have a choice between yes, no, and automatic integration, if necessary.

Width/Height: Width and height of the iframe in percentage or pixels can be specified.

Auto Height: Should the height be automatically adjusted?

Auto Add: By default, an http:// is inserted before an URL, if no http:// or https:// is found. This function can be turned on and off here.

Polls
Here the functionality for the display of polls is switched on or off. The polls themselves are configured in the polls component (see Section 4.7.6). You can decide here whether the content of the module should be cached or not.

Who's Online
The Who's Online module indicates who is currently on the site. A distinction is made between guests and registered users:

Figure 4.120: Who's
Online Module

The parameters for this module include:

Display: Here you decide on the display of the module. You have a choice between:

- Number of guests, number of users
- User names of the registered users
- A combination of the two choices shown above

Random Image:

Figure 4.121: Random
Image Module

With this module, selected randomized pictures from a file can be displayed in the order of your choice. This module is activated by default, but not assigned to any pages. Before you can see it on your site, you must assign the desired pages by clicking the edit icon. The parameters for this module include:

Image Type: Here you can specify the type of picture (.jpg, .png, or .gif). You can specify only one type at a time.

Image Folder: Here you have to enter the directory in which the pictures are stored. I have selected /images/stories.

Link: If you enter a URL here, the picture becomes clickable. The link target is the URL that you have specified here.

Width (px)/Height (px): Width and height of the displayed pictures in pixels. If you specify nothing here, the pictures are displayed according to the default.

Newsflash

The Newsflash module shows random hooks from dynamic content:

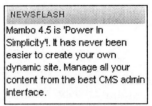

Figure 4.122: Newsflash
Module

The parameters for this module are:

Category: Here you can specify, by selection from a list, whether content items are to come from a special category or from all categories.

Style: Here you can select between a column representation (horizontal) and the vertical representation shown in Figure 4.123.

Show images: Should pictures that are contained in content be displayed or not?

Linked Titles: If you set item titles to Yes, you can specify here whether this title should be linked to the content page.

Read More: Integrate the read more link.

Item Title: Here you can decide whether you want to integrate the title of the (news) message.

No. of Items: Here you determine the number of pieces of content to be displayed at the same time.

Enable Cache: Should the content be cached?

Latest News

With this module the latest (newest) messages are displayed (Figure 4.123). By default, this is placed at the user1 position. You can also put it in another position, for example, to the right.

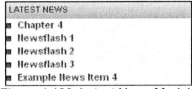
Figure 4.123: Latest News Module

The parameters for this module include:

Module Mode: Here you can decide whether you want to show dynamic (*content items only*), or static content (*static content items only*), or both, in the list.

Frontpage Items: When you are in the content items only mode, you can specify whether elements from the front page should also be included here.

Count: Here you determine the number of elements that can be displayed.

Category ID: If you enter the record numbers of the categories that are to be displayed, separated by commas, you force content to be selected from only these categories.

Section ID: Here you can enter the record numbers of the sections that are to be displayed, separated by commas. Thereby, the content selection is made only from these sections.

Popular

The most popular messages are displayed with this module.

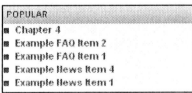
Figure 4.124: Popular Module

Search

The Search module appears only as an input field in the standard template:

search...

Figure 4.125: Search Module

The parameters for this module are:

Box Width: Size of the text box in characters: at the moment, it is 30 characters.

Text: Here you enter the text that is displayed in the search field.

Search Button: Here you can decide whether you want to have a search button or not.

Button Position: If you selected a search button, you can specify the position here (right, left, above, and below).

Button Text: Here you decide on the description of the search button.

4.8.3 Copying a Module

Imagine that you wish to display two different random pictures. One module should display pictures from listing A and a second module pictures from listing B. In such a case, you simply select the random images module by marking the check box before the name and click Copy.

A new module with the name of Copy of Random Image appears in the list. Change the settings as you desire and you have a new module:

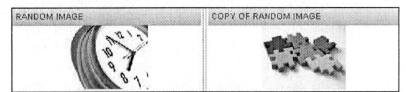

Figure 4.126: Copying of a Module

If you deactivate the Latest News and Popular modules, and put the two picture modules in the positions user1 and user2, the new modules are displayed in the content area of the template above the messages, and/or the front page.

4.8.4 Administrator Modules

Under the menu option Modules | Administrator Modules, you can see the Module Manager with the same structure. This time, however, modules are applied within the administration area:

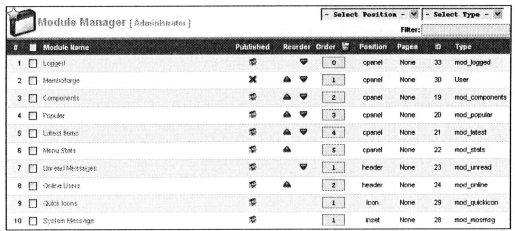

Figure 4.127: Administrator Module

Logged

This module shows a list of the currently logged-in users at the position cpanel, that is, as a tab in the Control Panel.

Mamboforge

The Mamboforge module shows the last message of the page `mamboforge.net` as an additional tab in the Control Panel:

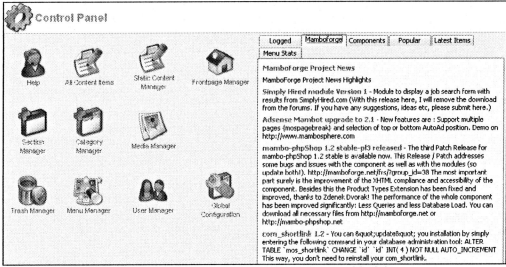

Figure 4.128: Mamboforge Administrator Module

Components
The components module lists the installed components as a tab in the control panel.

Popular
The popular module presents a list of the most visited content items as a tab in the control panel.

Latest Items
The latest items module offers a list of newest content items as a tab in the control panel.

Menu Stats
The menu stats module displays statistics about the allocation of the individual menu elements as a tab in the control panel.

Unread Messages
The unread messages module informs you about the number of unread administrator messages in the place header, that is, the top right.

Online Users
The online users' module indicates the number of logged-in users in the place header.

Quick Icons
The quick icons module offers icons for fast access in the control panel.

System Message

The system message module is responsible for the display of system messages.

Pathway
The pathway module is responsible for the display of the paths.

Toolbar
The toolbar module determines whether to display the toolbar.

Full Menu
The full menu module is responsible for the display of the Mambo Administration menu.

4.9 Mambots Menu

Bot is a short form for the word robot. A Mambot thus is a kind of Mambo robot. One can compare Mambots with a Mambo-specific script language. When we inserted pictures into content elements, we already came into contact with four built-in Mambots.

Mambots are always of a certain type. For example, in order to position the picture in the content element, you wrote {mosimage} in the text. This calls the `mos_image` Mambot during the representation of the page, which ensures that the assigned picture is shown.

4.9.1 Install New Mambots

New Mambots are installed in exactly the same manner as components, templates, and language files, via the menu option Mambots | Install Mambots—either by uploading or via directory installation.

4.9.2 Site Mambots

In the Mambot Manager, you will find nine *Content*, four *Editor*, and six *Search* Mambots:

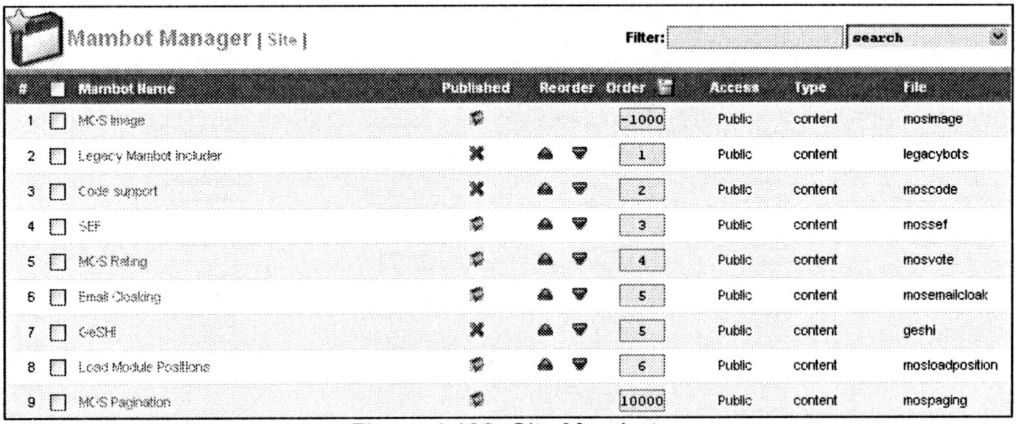

#		Mambot Name	Published	Reorder	Order	Access	Type	File
1	☐	MOS Image	✓		-1000	Public	content	mosimage
2	☐	Legacy Mambot includer	✗	▲ ▼	1	Public	content	legacybots
3	☐	Code support	✗	▲ ▼	2	Public	content	moscode
4	☐	SEF	✓	▲ ▼	3	Public	content	mossef
5	☐	MOS Rating	✓	▲ ▼	4	Public	content	mosvote
6	☐	Email Cloaking	✓	▲ ▼	5	Public	content	mosemailcloak
7	☐	GeSHi	✗	▲ ▼	5	Public	content	geshi
8	☐	Load Module Positions	✓	▲ ▼	6	Public	content	mosloadposition
9	☐	MOS Pagination	✓		10000	Public	content	mospaging

Figure 4.129: Site Mambots

Mambots have few to no changeable settings, since they are mostly programmed and optimized for a very special purpose.

MOS Image (content): This Mambot displays the picture in the content elements on the site with the command {mosimage} (see Section 4.6.3).

Legacy Mambot (content): The Legacy Mambot offers support for older Mambots from version 4.5 onwards.

Code Support (content): The Code Support Mambot formats source code; thus content elements that contain source code can be formatted, with the command {moscode}.

Listing 4.2: Deployment of the moscode Mambot

```
<code>{moscode}
if ($number > 0){
echo $number;
} else{
$number++;
}
{/moscode}</code>
```

SEF (content): SEF stands for **Search Engine-Friendly**. This Mambot produces the search engine-friendly URLs for content elements. If you use the associated feature, this Mambot must be activated.

MOS Rating (content): This is the Mambot that provides the evaluation bar about the content. If you want to use this, it must be activated.

E-mail Cloaking (content): This Mambot changes an e-mail address that you have entered into a content element in the form of hagen@sit2000.de:

```
<a href=mailto:hagen@sit2000.de> hagen@sit2000.de</a>
```

GeSHi (content): The GeSHi Mambot formats source code like moscode. GeSHI, however, understands syntax highlighting and provides impressive listings on the site, if you merge the source code to be formatted into < pre > </pre > HTML tags. The GeSHi Mambot, which structures and colors the code, therefore highlights the source code:

```
if ($number > 0) {
        echo $number;
}       else{
        $number++;
}
```

Figure 4.130: With GeSHi-
formatted Source Code

Listing 4.3: Deployment of the GeSHi Mambot

```
<pre>
if ($number > 0){
echo $number;
} else{
$number++;
}
</pre>
```

Load Module (content): The Load Module Mambot makes it possible to load modules within content. It is called with {mosloadposition user1}, for example.

MOS Pagination (content): The MOS Pagination Mambot takes care of page breaks in content elements. It is simply inserted into content in the same way as the MOS Images Mambot. Besides a simple word wrap, you can also define various headings and lemmas.

Syntax:

```
{mospagebreak}
{mospagebreak title=page title}
{mospagebreak heading=first page}
{mospagebreak title=page title titleheading=first page}
{mospagebreak heading=first page title=page title}
```

No WYSIWYG Editor/TinyMCE WYSIWYG Editor (Editor): You can control the activation of these two Mambots via Site | Global Configuration. Thus the WYSIWYG editor is activated in many description texts.

MOS Image Editor Button/MOS Pagebreak Editor Button (Editor-XTD): These two Mambots generate the two buttons below the editor. By clicking on these buttons, a {mosimage} or a {mospagebreak} is inserted into the text.

Search Mambots
The Search Mambots for content, web links, contacts, categories, sections, and news feeds can be activated as needed. They influence the behavior of the search module.

4.10 Installers Menu

All installers are summarized in the Installers menu:

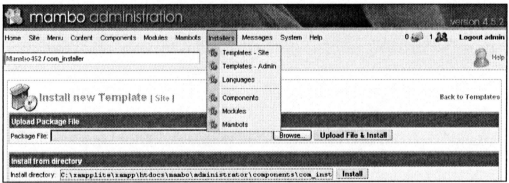

Figure 4.131: Installers

The menu branches out to installers for:

- Site templates
- Admin templates
- Languages
- Components
- Modules
- Mambots

4.11 Messages Menu

The messages menu manages administrator messages. Mambo has a small communication network that enables sending of messages within the administrators group. In addition, system messages are also delivered; for example, if someone has posted a new content element.

4.11.1 Inbox

The messages are collected for you here. By clicking the new icon, you can send a new message to users who are permitted access to Mambo administration.

4.11.2 Configuration

Here you can configure the communication system.

Lock Inbox: You can lock your mailbox and thus suppress the receipt of messages. This is OK if you are the only administrator; otherwise you should leave your inbox open.

Mail me a new Message: This feature is really useful. Mambo sends the messages to the e-mail address given in the user administration.

4.12 System Menu

The system menu consists of only one element. This is a global checking-in of all content elements in process.

4.12.1 Global Check-In

If an entitled user calls up the editing mode of a content element, then this element is checked out. Only the entitled user may work on this element. During processing, other users will see a lock icon in front of the name of the element. If the document is stored after the change, it is then automatically checked in again and the lock icon disappears.

If the user closes his or her browser window, or if there is a sudden break in their Internet connection, the element remains checked out and cannot be changed any more.

Here the Global Check-In comes into play. By clicking this menu option, all elements in process are checked in and you receive an appropriate list of the elements:

Database Table	# of items	Checked in
Checking table - mos_banner	Checked in 0 items	
Checking table - mos_bannerclient	Checked in 1 items	✔
Checking table - mos_categories	Checked in 0 items	
Checking table - mos_contact_details	Checked in 0 items	
Checking table - mos_content	Checked in 0 items	
Checking table - mos_mambots	Checked in 0 items	
Checking table - mos_menu	Checked in 0 items	
Checking table - mos_modules	Checked in 0 items	
Checking table - mos_newsfeeds	Checked in 0 items	
Checking table - mos_polls	Checked in 0 items	
Checking table - mos_sections	Checked in 0 items	
Checking table - mos_weblinks	Checked in 0 items	
Checked out items have now been all checked in		

Figure 4.132: Global Check-in

The disadvantage of global checking-in is the fact that all elements get checked in. If someone is just about to change something, this element is also checked in and someone else can also change it. Be careful with this function and pay attention to who is online.

Now that we know how to customize Mambo to our specific needs, we can concentrate on extending our website using a wide range of Mambo extensions.

5

Useful Extensions

We have reached the almost inexhaustible range of Mambo extensions. As beautiful as the standard version is, soon you will be searching for components, modules, and Mambots with which you can extend your website. Due to the modular structure of Mambo, it is easy to create extensions. The following are six popular extensions:

- A forum
- A calendar
- A picture gallery for photographs
- The ability to post comments
- Creating multilingual pages
- An online shop

The website `http://www.mamboforge.net` contains lots of components, modules, Mambots, templates, and language files that you may require.

> The scope for creating additional extensions exists, but commercial extensions are also available. Before you buy one of these, you should carefully assess your requirements and check out modules suitable for your application. You can also take part in the further development of these modules.

5.1 Forum

Forums are used to display and administer a number of topics where users with common interests can post messages. Such a forum is called a **board**. A good board is the component from *Two Shoes Mambo Factory* (`http://tsmf.net/`) with the descriptive name of **Simpleboard**.

5.1.1 What can Simpleboard do?

For non-English speaking users, the biggest problem with open-source software is that often no manual is provided in a local language. Due to this, there is no overview of the functions offered by the software. One should gain as much information about the software as possible, before installing it. The following functions are available for the different types of users:

Simpleboard administrator functions include:

- Full integration into Mambo administration.
- Changing user profiles: The forum component recognizes users that have an account in the website. A profile is automatically created the first time the user visits the forum. Every user can create a forum profile by means of his/her user details.
- Adding access rights to forums.
- Editing posts and viewing previous posts of a topic.
- Specifying a minimum time span between posts to secure the forum from flood attacks.
- Forum categories for building a structure with an overview.
- Customizing appearance with the CSS template editor.

The administrator functions available directly from the forum include:

- Modifying, deleting, and moving posts
- Locking and unlocking topics (that is, preventing further posts to a topic)
- Positioning a topic at the beginning of the topic list

The functions for all visitors include:

- Writing of posts
- Use of smileys and BBCode for text formatting without knowledge of HTML
- Two different views of the posts (flat or threaded)

The functions for registered users are:

- Private user profile
- E-mail notifications of new posts in a topic
- Creating a signature that can be automatically added to every post
- Uploading files and pictures to a post

5.1.2 Installation of Simpleboard

Download the com_simpleboard-1.0.4-beta2.zip file. Click Installer | Components in the menu bar. Scan your computer for the file and click Upload File & Install. The installer loads the package onto your server, unpacks the individual files, adds the necessary tables to the database, and then gives you further information:

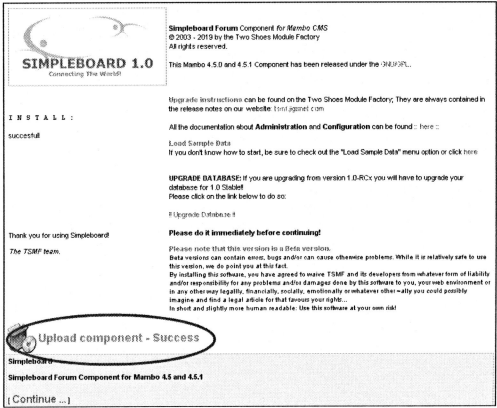

Figure 5.1: Successful Installation of the Forum Component

That's it! The component is installed when you see the Upload component – Success message. The database tables have been created and your Mambo administration has been customized accordingly. Click Continue, thank the Mambo development team for this wonderful installer, and thank *Two Shoes Mambo Factory* for their forum! In the Mambo administration you can see the new component—the Simpleboard forum.

Uninstallation

Select the component and click Uninstall. The component and data are now permanently deleted.

5.1.3 Simpleboard Administration

After installation, there is a new entry in the Components menu. Click Components | Simpleboard and you will see the Control Panel of your forum component. There are eleven icons giving quick access to the forum features:

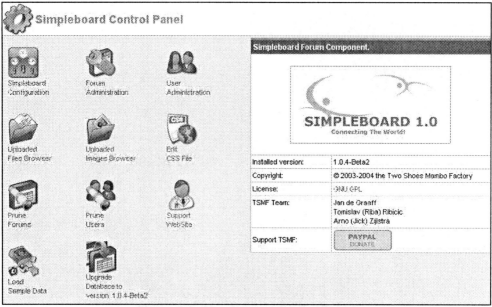

Figure 5.2: Simpleboard Control Panel

There is a PAYPAL button on the bottom right of the Control Panel. Try to make a small donation if you are satisfied with the forum. A lot of work has been invested in such components, and programmers have to eat and pay the rent! They are pleased when someone acknowledges their work.

It is possible to install a different language file in this component; the entire forum administration thereafter appears in the chosen language. If you choose German, for example, you need to upload the german-SB1.0.4-beta2.zip file and unpack it. You have to copy the file into the subdirectory [Mambo]/administrator/components /com_simpleboard/language/ by hand. Now everything depends on your installation.

If you followed the examples in the book, you have already customized a German Mambo version during global configuration. Your global language file is called germanf.php. In order to harmonize the forum and Mambo, you also have to rename the forum language file to germanf.php. After renaming, you will see the forum in the German language. The translation to German is an unnerving mixture of German and

English, which really makes me wonder whether one really should translate administration interfaces. You be the judge!

Simpleboard Configuration

Here you specify the basic configuration of your Simpleboard component:

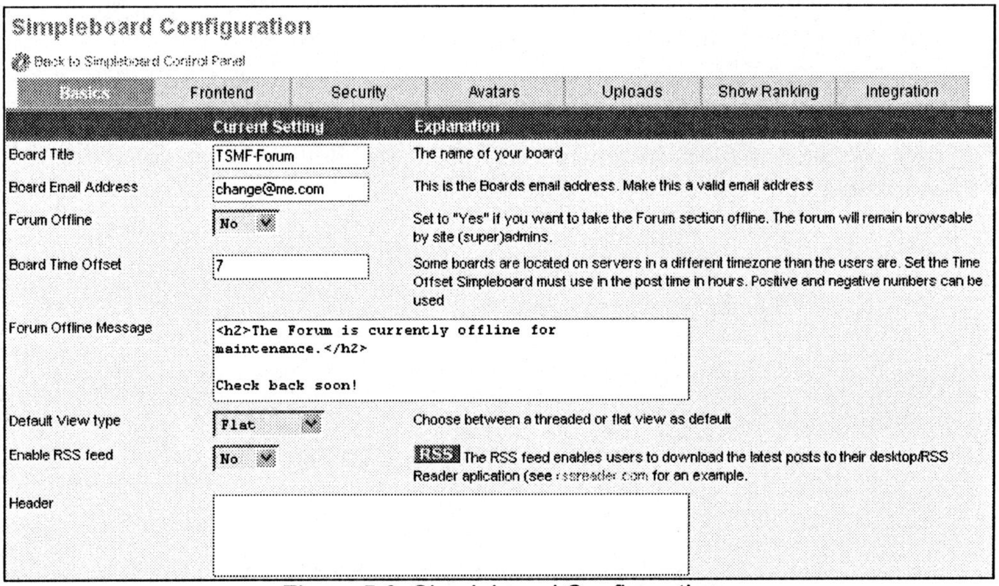

Figure 5.3: Simpleboard Configuration

Descriptions of the seven tabs that run along the top of this screen are as follows:

Basics
Enter a Board Title and your Board Email Address. A bit like Mambo itself, you can disable the forum and supply an appropriate message in Forum Offline Message.

With Board Time Offset, you can change the time base.

In Default View type, you chose from the two possible views for forum postings (Flat or Threaded).

In Enable RSS feed you can add an RSS button on the forum page. This creates an XML file for a news feed of the newest forum posts.

Enter a Header so that it appears in the header area of the forum.

Frontend
There are four blocks of parameters for changing the 'look and feel' of the forum. You can stick with the standard settings, or you can enable or disable display areas, and specify many other useful things.

Security

By default, the board is set up so every visitor can read and write. Flood protection is disabled and a moderator is sent an e-mail whenever a new post is added. You can leave the default settings as they are.

Avatars

Avatars are small pictures that can be attached to a user and displayed alongside his or her posts in the forum. A library of existing pictures is available and you can make changes to settings related to user upload, physical size of images, and file sizes.

Uploads

Each user can upload a file and/or picture with each post. Both are displayed with the user's post. In this tab, you can adjust what exactly you want to permit. You should also add PDFs to the permitted file types.

Show Ranking

Depending on their number of posts, each user is given a particular name and picture. Thus, other visitors can differentiate 'beginners' from 'net-heads'. In this tab, you set up the names of the individual stages and the number of posts it takes to move up a rank.

Integration

Here you can integrate various components into Simpleboard. For example, the Discussion Mambot enables a comment link and adds an appropriate entry into the text of the content element.

You can post a comment after opening the content elements. This comment is treated like a topic in a forum and you can skillfully shift discussions about content into the forum.

Forum Administration

Here you set up forums and forum categories. Click New and you will see a form with three tabs:

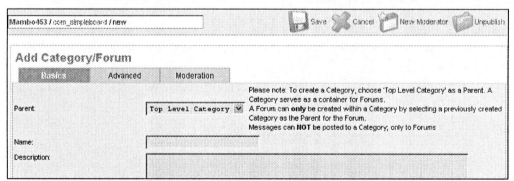

Figure 5.4: Add Forums and Categories

Basics: Before setting up a forum, you have to create a category, let's say with the name Cafeteria, and give a basic description for it.

Advanced: Here you specify the access rights for the category.

Moderation: This tab does not affect categories, but is available as this form is used for creating categories and forums. Save the category by clicking Save and this category will show up as unpublished in your overview:

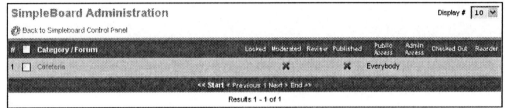

Figure 5.5: New Category

Repeat the procedure to create another forum. Call it Tips & Tricks and enter a description. Select the recently created Cafeteria as the assigned category. Click Save.

There are now two entries in your overview. Publish both by clicking Publish and the basic version of your forum is completed:

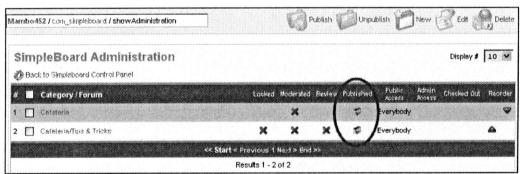

Figure 5.6: Publication of a New Forum

Merge the newly created forum with the main menu, so users can get there via a link from your website.

Click Menu | Main menu and then New. In the following dialog, select Component, as shown in Figure 5.7, and click Next. Name the new menu entry as Forum and select Simpleboard forum in the component list. Keep the access as Public and click Save:

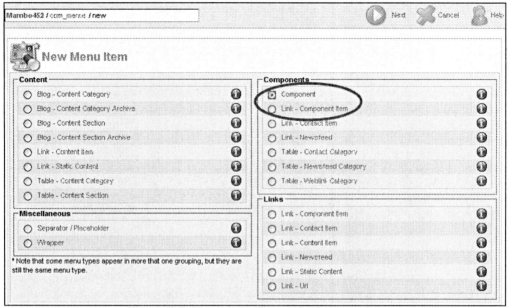

Figure 5.7: New Menu Entry of a Component

If you go to your website and reload the page, there will be a new entry entitled Forum at the bottom of the main menu. Click on it to start your new component:

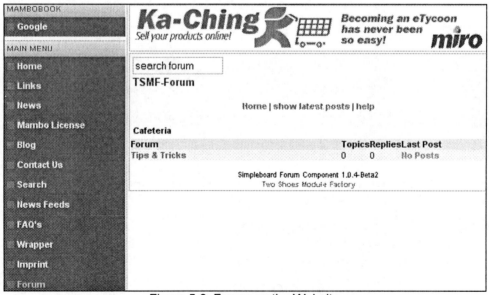

Figure 5.8: Forum on the Website

If you see an error message, you'll have to modify the source code. Open the /components/com_simpleboard/simpleboard.php file with a text editor. In line forty-eight, check the version number of Mambo. As you know, our Simpleboard is a beta version. When it was released, there was apparently no Mambo version 4.5.2, only Mambo 4.5.1b.

For Mambo version 4.5.2, add the following line:

```
} elseif ( $mambo_release == "4.5" && ($mambo_dev_level == "1" ||
$mambo_dev_level == "1a" || $mambo_dev_level == "2") ){
```

The value of mambo_dev_level, the version number, is the crucial item in this code. Since we are using version 4.5.2 there should be a 2 at the end. For version 4.5.3, you would add a 3. Save this file and load it on your server via FTP.

You have now programmed using PHP. It isn't that difficult, is it?

User Administration

Here you can change existing user profiles. The list is still empty. Create a profile (see Section 5.1.4) or write a post so you'll have a few entries in the list:

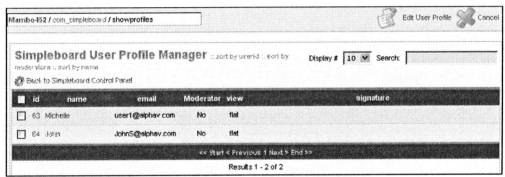

Figure 5.9: Simpleboard User Profile Manager

You can work on profiles by clicking the Edit User Profile icon.

File Browser

In the file browser, you can administer the uploaded files that users attached to the postings. You can delete a file (Remove Completely) or jump to the appropriate post in the forum (Open Message):

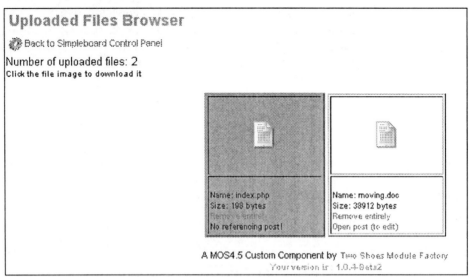

Figure 5.10: Simpleboard File Browser

Uploaded Images Browser

In the images browser, you can administer pictures that were uploaded for the posts. You have the same options as in the file browser (see Figure 5.10).

Edit CSS File

Like Mambo, the forum also contains templates. You can modify the appropriate CSS file from Mambo administration:

Figure 5.11: Simpleboard Template CSS Editor

You can find additional templates on the *Two Shoes Mambo Factory* website.

Prune Forums

Forums exist for discussions. They are not productive when there are many topics but few answers. The Cut Forums function enables you to delete topics that have no responses. You have to select the forum and the number of days you want it to remain active.

Prune User

This function synchronizes the users of the Mambo user administration with those of the Simpleboard component. For example, when users are deleted in Mambo, they are also deleted in Simpleboard after applying this function.

Support WebSite

You can find various forums, downloads, and items of news about the forum component at the *Two Shoes Mambo Factory* website.

Load Sample Data

Clicking this button loads sample data into your forum. Sample data is always useful for practice. This function is only available after installation. You can also find a link to the sample data on the web page that appears after installation (see Figure 5.1).

Update Database to Version 1.0.4-Beta2:

If you have installed an older version of Simpleboard, you can update your database structure by clicking on this icon. As we are using the latest version of Simpleboard, we will get the following message:

Simpleboard tables could not be upgraded. It appears they are already at the latest version.

5.1.4 User Frontend

Visitors can post topics when you have merged the forum with your website (see Section 5.1.3).

By default, a new forum is left empty, which can be confusing for inexperienced users. You can start working on this new forum by posting a greeting message. The first post is the topic (Caption).

The integrated editor is unfortunately not Mambo's WYSIWYG editor, but an editor based on **Bulletin Board Code (BBCode)**. This code is an unofficial standard on web forums.

First click on the Forum link in the main menu, then on Tips & Tricks in the forum list, and finally on the Create new caption. You can write a posting in the form that pops up on your screen:

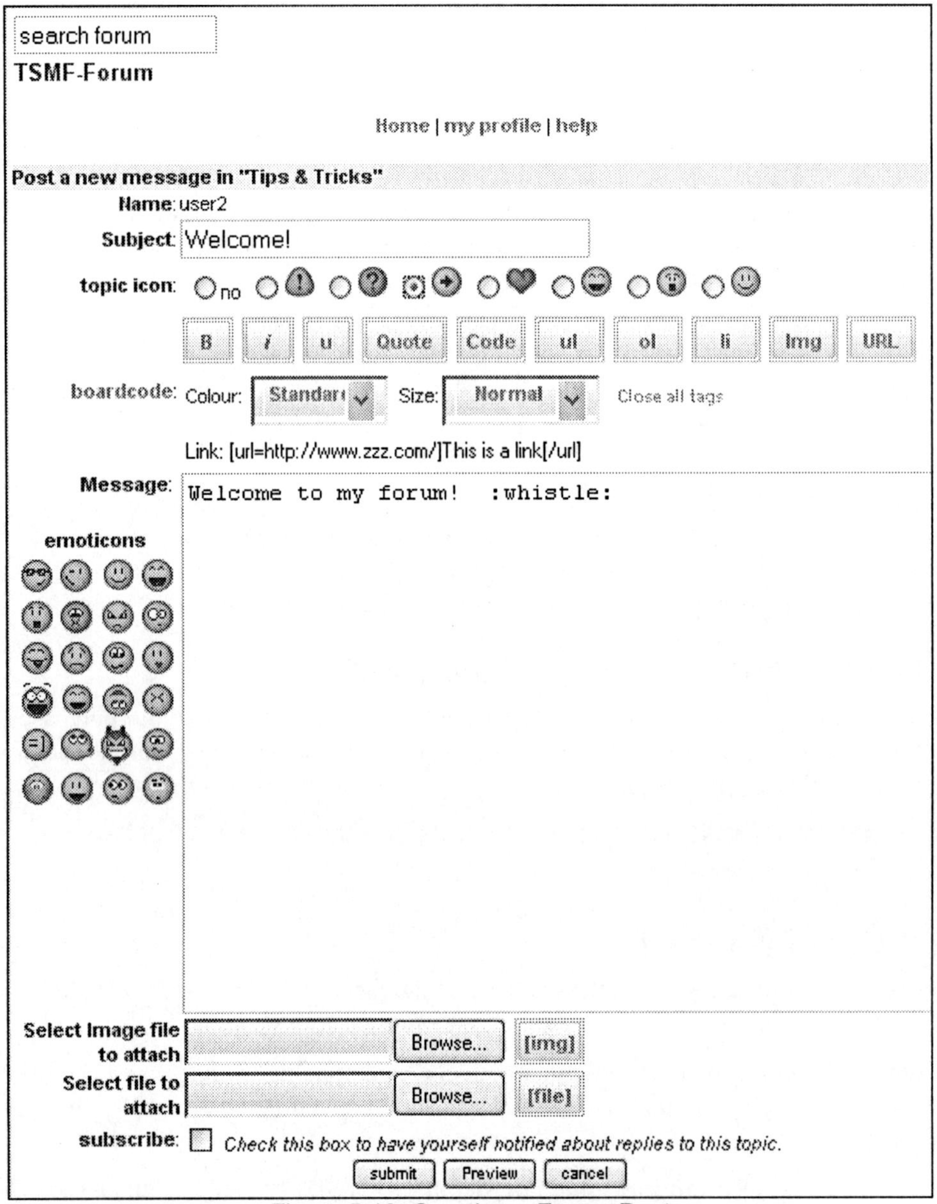

Figure 5.12: Creating a Forum Post

The buttons with letters correspond to the HTML tags of the same name:

- B – bold
- i – italic
- u – underline
- Quote – quote from another posting
- Code – code
- ul – unordered list
- ol – ordered list
- li – list item
- Img – image
- URL – Link

If you move your mouse over the buttons, the text directly above the text area field changes and the help text related to the button is displayed. You can add a picture and/or a file to your post by entering the path in the appropriate input field. There is a subscribe check box below this field. Check it if you want to be notified by e-mail about responses to your post.

Click submit after you have entered some text in the editor. The post is stored and you have the option of moving on to different places of the forum via links. After a few seconds, the program will redirect to your post:

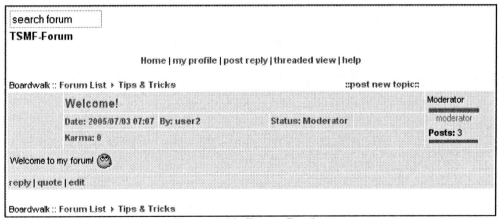

Figure 5.13: Forum Posting

All users including you can respond to this post. Write a short response, perhaps under another user name. The new post is displayed under your first post. If you click Tips & Tricks, you will wind up in the topic overview (Topics) and your first heading will be a Welcome! greeting:

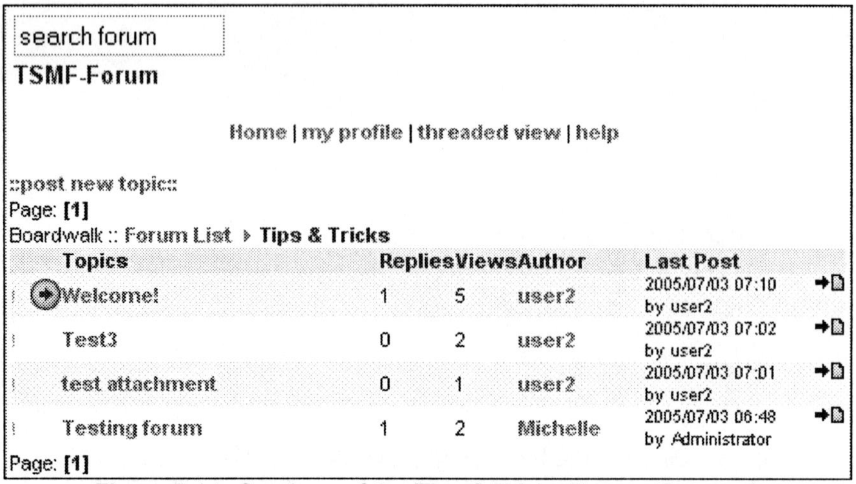

Figure 5.14: Captions of the Tips & Tricks Forum (flat view)

Here you can see that users have accessed this post five times and there is a response to it. The last response was written by user2 on 2005/07/03 at 07:10.

In the link bar above the forum there is a link reading flat view or threaded view. Flat view shows the number of replies, views, and the most recent post in one row. However, in threaded view, the Topics column contains hyperlinked titles that indicate the relationship of replies to the parent post. This overview has a tree structure, which uses more space, but it is easier to follow the replies to the parent post:

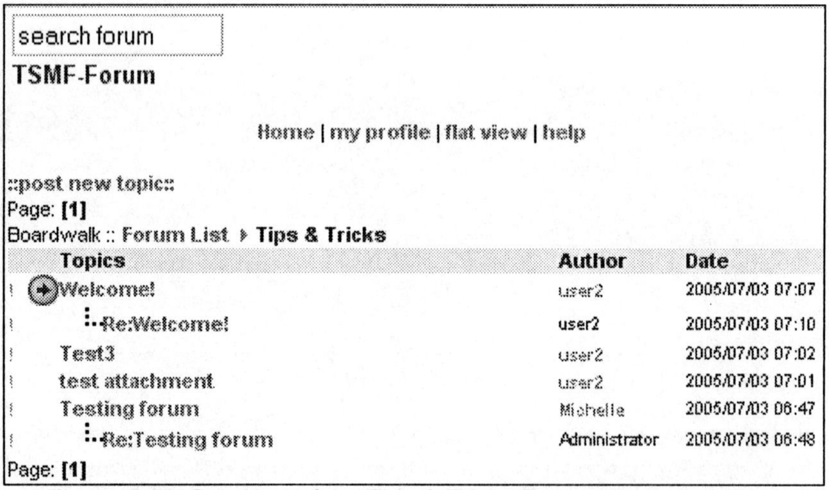

Figure 5.15: Captions of the Tips & Tricks Forum (threaded view)

See how the display changes when you click each of these links.

Set Up a User Profile

Open the forum on your website, click my profile, and fill it as you wish.

Preferred view: Select flat or threaded view.

Ordering: Specify how the messages should be ordered.

Signature: Define the text that will be automatically inserted at the end of your posts.

Avatar: Upload a picture or choose one from the list of available avatars:

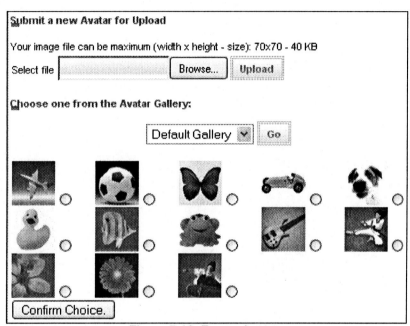

Figure 5.16: Forum Avatars

5.1.5 Simpleboard Module

Naturally, there are modules available for the Simpleboard component. For example, there is a module that displays the last five forum postings on your website.

Installation

Download the mod_simpleboard5.zip file and install it by clicking Installers | Modules. After installation, a new module named mod_simpleboard appears in the module list. By clicking Modules | Site Modules, you can name the new module and determine the pages on which it is to be displayed. In this example, it is called 'forum posts' and is published on all pages on the right side of the template area. The last five forum posts are displayed on the web page:

Figure 5.17: Simpleboard
Module

5.2 Calendar

A calendar is useful for websites where many appointments are scheduled, for instance. There is a popular component available for Mambo with the unspectacular name **Events** (http://events.mamboforge.net/).

5.2.1 Installation

Download the com_events-1.2.zip file and install it from the menu option Installers | Components. You will receive a message that the component has been installed:

New demo web site for Events Calendar. Check out http://mosevents.sourceforge.net
ATTENTION
Please open Components :: Events :: Edit config
and change the Admin email address!
Then, open Components :: Events :: Manage events categories
and set up your categories. You have to set up and publish at least one before you can add any event.

This is followed by further instructions. In addition, a new component named Events appears in the component list.

5.2.2 Configuration

Click Components | Events. You will see three menu entries: Manage events, Manage event categories, and Events config.

Events Config

Here you can specify the admin's e-mail address, determine which users can post events, format the date and time, and customize the layout. The first tab handles the parameters for the component:

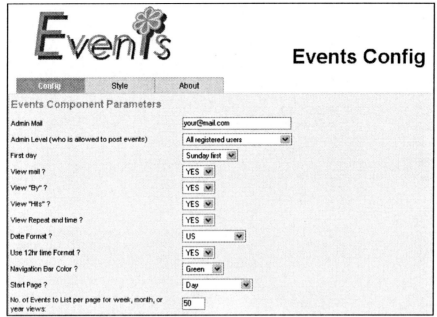

Figure 5.18: Event Component Parameters

Admin Mail: Change the e-mail address to your own.

Admin Level: Specify whether registered or special users are allowed to post events.

First day: Specify the day (Sunday or Monday) from where the week should begin.

View mail ?, View "By" ?, View "Hits" ?, View Repeat and Time ?: Assign various display options for individual appointments.

Date Format ?: Change the format of the date if required. I use a format that displays in the following way: Sunday, 27 March 2005.

Use 12hr time Format: Chose between the twelve-hour and twenty-four-hour clock.

Navigation Bar Color ?: Select the color of the navigation bar.

Start Page ?: Select the type of display that is to be default for the calendar (day, week, month, year, monthly list, categories, or a search field).

No. of Events to List per page for week, month, or year views: Enter the number of events that are to be displayed on the first page of the list.

The second tab, Style, contains a CSS editor for customizing the layout. A button here lets you enter the default values back into the CSS file.

Manage Event Categories

Before entering an event, you need a category. Go to Components | Manage event categories in the menu bar and click New:

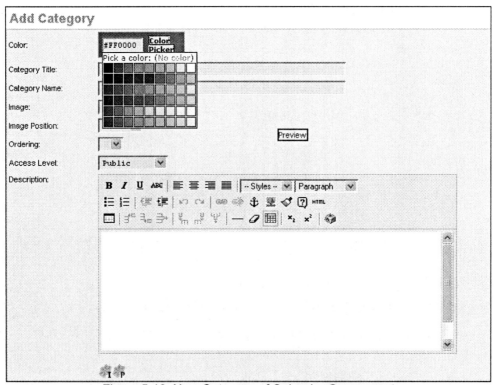

Figure 5.19: New Category of Calendar Component

You can set up a category here. Each category has a different color so it is easier to recognize in the calendar. In addition, you can assign and position a picture from the Media Manager. You can also upload a picture on the spot just by clicking the upload icon. The picture is saved in the /images/stories/ subdirectory. You can add a description for the components using the WYSIWYG editor. After you finish editing, click Save to store your changes.

Once this is done, you still have to publish the category in the Events Category Manager.

Manage Events

This allows you to enter your preferences. Click Components | Events | Manage events in the menu bar, and then click New. You will see a form with four tabs:

Events: Here you specify a title, a category, and a description for the event. The WYSIWYG editor is again at your disposal to help with the description. You can also set up a place, a contact, and some additional information:

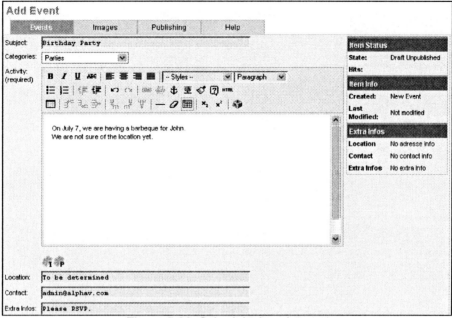

Figure 5.20: Schedule Appointment

Images: Here you can assign a picture from the Media Manager to the event just as for Content Items:

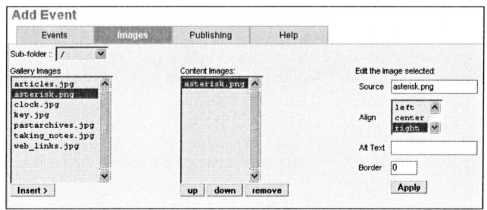

Figure 5.21: Assign Picture

Publishing: It is easy to enter the dates of events. Click on the button with three dots and a calendar pops up. Here you can select the first and last day of the event:

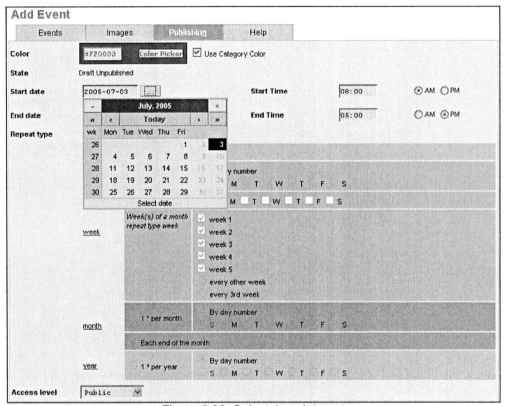

Figure 5.22: Select Appointment

In addition, you can scroll through months and years by clicking on the «/» symbols.

The Start Time and End Time has to be entered in a twelve-hour or twenty-four-hour format (hh:mm) depending on the settings in Event Config.

Another convenient feature is the repeat options for appointments:

Every day: Select this option for an event that is repeated on one other or several days. A new event will be entered for each of the days with the same start and end time.

Every week: This option makes it possible to choose the day of the week on which the event takes place.

Several days in one week: This option lists several events that occur on different days of the week. Weeks: With this option, you can repeat events based on weeks, for example, every two weeks.

Month: Here you can select a day of the month for the repeat with this option.

At the end of the month: The event is on the last day of every month as long as the last day falls in the period specified by the start and end date.

Year: This option lets you select a day of the year to repeat the event.

Help: In this tab, specifications of the event-date are explained in detail. One-day events that extend beyond midnight can be set up here.

Be careful with the special case of a one-day event that ends after midnight. When a one-day event begins, for example, at 19:00 and ends at 3:00, the start and end dates must be set for the same date and for the date before midnight.

To show a link to the calendar from the site, you have to merge the calendar component into the main menu. Click Menu | Main menu and New, select Component in the subsequent dialog, and then click Next (see Figure 5.7).

Name the new menu as Calendar and select Events in the component list. Leave the access as Public and click Save.

If you reload your website, there should be a new entry at the bottom of your main menu (Calendar). Clicking on it will start the new component:

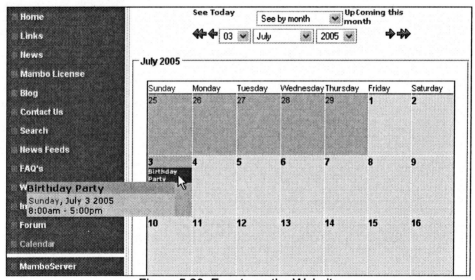

Figure 5.23: Events on the Website

5.2.3 User Frontend

When you log in to the website, you may or may not enter appointments depending on the settings in Event Config.

If you have permission, two links appear below the calendar: enter appointments and my appointments.

Behind the enter appointments link there is the same interface as in Mambo administration, inclusive of help text. Behind the my appointments link, you can see the appointments that you have entered under this user name. Next to each is a Modify and Delete link:

Figure 5.24: Your Appointments on the Website

Click on the event name to see a corresponding form displaying the details of the event. To modify the form, click on the highlighted pencil icon:

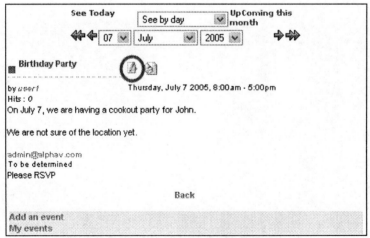

Figure 5.25: Appointment with Editor Icon

5.2.4 Module

For the Event component, a module displays the current month on the website.

Download the mod_events_cal-1.1-beta.zip file and install it from the menu option Installers | Modules. After the installation, a new module named mod_events_cal appears in the module list.

Click Modules | Site Modules, name the new module, and specify the pages on which it is to appear. In this example, it is called Appointments and is published on all the pages in the right side of the template area:

Figure 5.26: Event Module

The month is now displayed on the site with differently colored days indicating events.

5.2.5 Event Mambot

The Event Mambot is always ready to browse appointments via the search module.

Download the bot_events_search-1.1.zip file and call it up from the menu bar by clicking Installers. Select the file and click Upload File & Install button. Search Events shows up in the list of installed Mambots.

Click Mambots | Site Mambots in the menu bar and publish the newly installed Event Mambot.

When you now enter something in the search field of your website, appointments and events are also searched and are shown in the results list if a match is found.

5.3 Gallery

You often find pictures, sculptures, montages, and similar artistic works in a gallery. In principle, a gallery is a collection of images. The Internet is becoming more visually rich nowadays and a picture, after all, says a thousand words.

There are many areas suitable for galleries. For example, if you want to create an association's website, you might want to photograph your association meetings and your members. Why not put these pictures at the disposal of the visitors or registered users of your site using a gallery?

5.3.1 Zoom Media Gallery

Mike de Boer from Rotterdam, Netherlands, developed this component. From his website (http://ummagumma.nl/mikedeboer/), you can download the current version, join in the discussion on the forum, and check out a demo of the component.

5.3.2 Zoom Media Gallery: Installation

Download the com_zoom_214_RC3.zip file and install it from the menu option Installers | Components. A message about where the component was installed, and instructions about how to make it work, is displayed after installation.

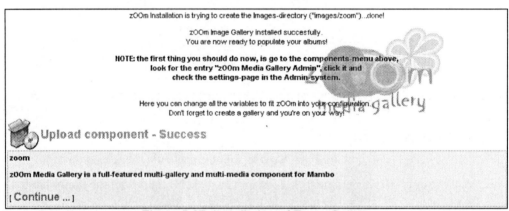

Figure 5.27: Installation of Zoom Gallery

Click Continue and you will see a new component with the name zOOm Media Gallery Admin in the component list.

5.3.3 Changing the Language

By default, this component is available only in English and Dutch (Version 2.1.4 RC3). If you choose to have everything in your local language, you need the appropriate language file. Download the zoom_media_gallery_2.1.4RC3.zip file and unpack it. Copy the language files to [mambo]/components/com_zoom/language/ on your computer and henceforth your Zoom Media Gallery will speak the local language.

5.3.4 Zoom Gallery: Administration

In the Components menu, you will find a new menu option zOOm Media Gallery Admin. The administration gallery consists of six icons displayed one below the other:

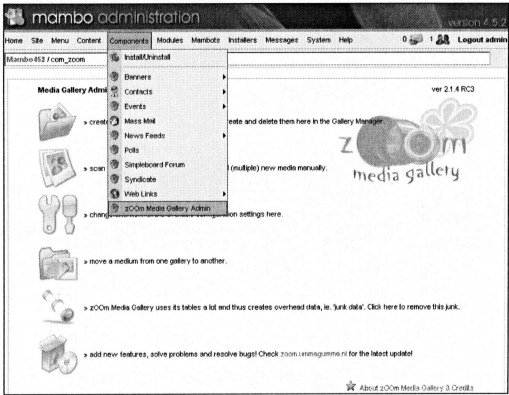

Figure 5.28: Administration

If you roll your mouse over the icons, a tooltip appears showing their name.

Gallery Manager

As is the case with all content, a certain order is necessary. For pictures, the hierarchical levels are called **galleries**. Click Gallery Manager and then New Gallery. The input form for a new gallery is divided into two tabs.

Properties
In the Properties tab, specify the properties of the gallery:

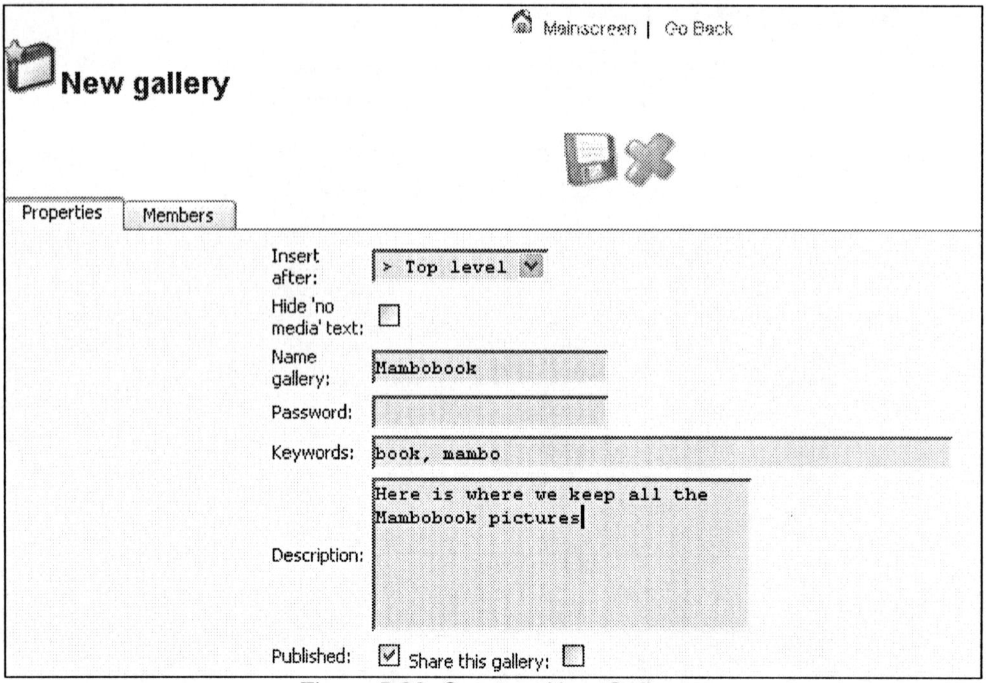

Figure 5.29: Create a New Gallery

The options available under Properties are:

Insert after: Just like the Mambo menu entry system, you can nest galleries to your liking. To do this, you must select the parent gallery here.

Hide 'no media' text: If there are no pictures in the gallery, the text no media is displayed. If you don't want this text, click the check box.

Name gallery: This is the name of the gallery that will appear on the website.

Keywords: These keywords are considered while searching.

Description: The description you entered is shown on the gallery's page.

Published: This is where you release the gallery.

Members
In the Members tab, you enter the access rights for the gallery.

Public Access: All users of the website can access the pictures.

Members Only: Only registered users can access the pictures.

User Name: Only the named user can access the pictures.

After clicking Save, you will see a message box indicating that the gallery has been created and you are automatically sent to the list of existing galleries. If you want to edit a gallery, select it via the check box and click Edit.

Upload Files

You can upload files in different ways.

single (ZIP-)file: Presumably, you will first want to upload an individual file. The principle is always the same. File location, gallery, name, keywords, and description text are specified as shown in the picture:

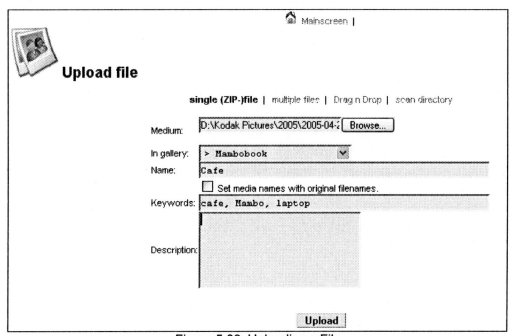

Figure 5.30: Uploading a File

multiple files: The form for individual files is shown several times so you can upload several pictures at once.

Drag n Drop: If you have the Java plug-in in your browser and/or have the Java Runtime Environment installed on your computer (http://java.sun.com/products/plugin/), you can start a Java applet with which you can transfer several files at once by clicking Drag n Drop:

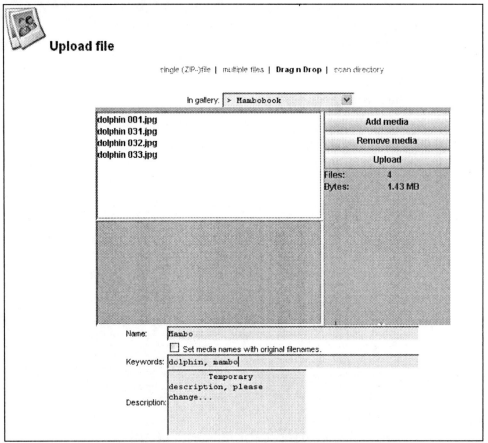

Figure 5.31: Java Applet for File Upload

With the Java applet you can also add files using a normal file dialog or via Drag n Drop from your File Manager. You have to assign the same description to all pictures.

scan directory: You can search whole directories for pictures and upload them together.

Settings

The settings dialog is divided into four tabs: System, Layout, Safe Mode, and Accessibility.

System

When working with pictures, issues that always crop up are size and overview. Having thumbnails (small picture previews) displayed a bit like a table of contents on a page has become standard on the Internet:

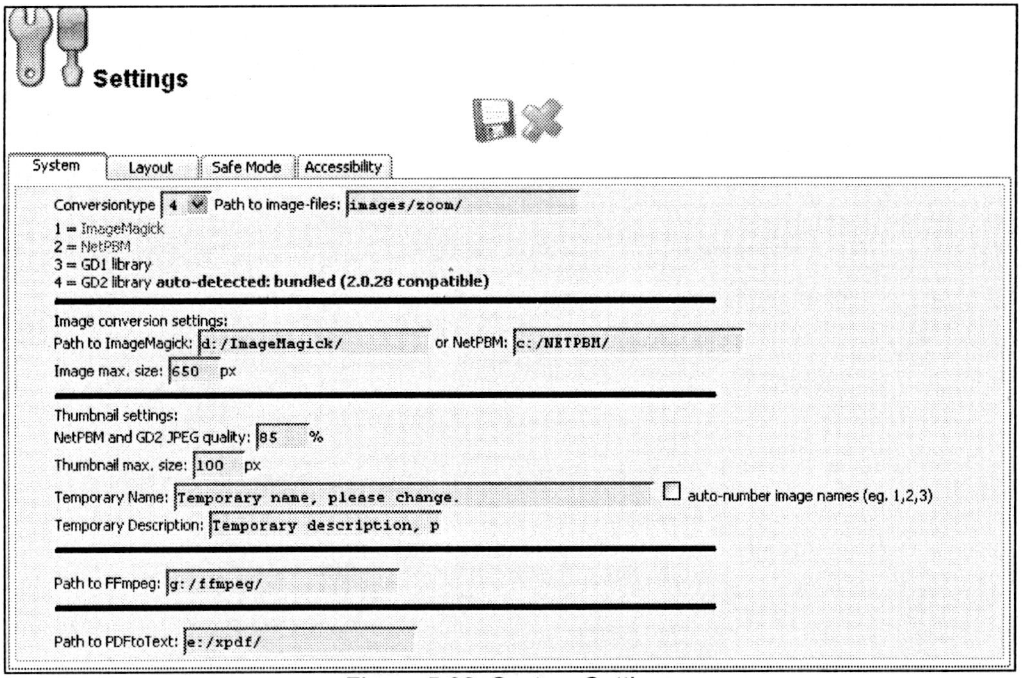

Figure 5.32: System Settings

The advantage is that users get a rough overview of the pictures without downloading them. By clicking on the preview of a picture, the corresponding large version is opened.

> Depending on your server configuration, it is possible that the multiple upload option will not work, but soon there will be a version that can do this error-free.

To do this, the preview pictures have to be produced automatically. It is not that simple and can be performed in several ways.

The Zoom Media Gallery offers four possibilities. Two external programs, ImageMagick (http://www.imagemagick.org/) and NetPBM (http://netpbm.sourceforge.net/) must be installed on the server, and two libraries, GD1 and GD2 must be compiled into the PHP module. Since you have no influence on the selection of the software installed on a rented server and both require major system resources, the first two options are just a matter of luck. With a local installation under Windows or Linux, you can download and install the programs yourself.

The third program, the GD library (http://www.boutell.com/gd/), has the advantage that it is already contained in PHP. There are different versions of PHP and GD.

Fortunately, the setup routine recognizes whether GD is the latest version and selects it automatically. GD has less functionality than the first two programs, but can produce .jpg previews.

NetPBM and GD2 JPEG quality: Here you specify the compression ratio as a percentage.

Thumbnail max. size: Here you determine the size of the preview picture in pixels.

Temporary Name: Here you type in a default name.

Temporary Description: Here you can specify a standard description.

Path to FFmpeg: ffmpeg is a command-line program that converts files from a video/audio or picture format into another format. It also supports recording and encoding from a TV card in real time.

Path to PDFtoText: A program that converts PDF to text.

Layout

Here you can specify various stylistic parameters for your gallery:

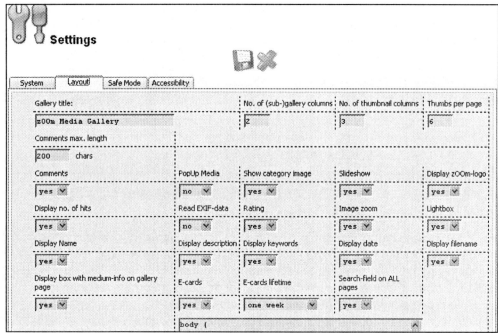

Figure 5.33: Layout Settings

The parameters decide the number of thumbnails on a page and the display or lack of display, for example, comments, postcards, keywords, search fields, etc.

In addition, the Zoom Media Gallery CSS file can be customized here and a method for sorting the thumbnails can be selected.

Safe Mode

The PHP language has a "safe mode" in which certain actions, for example file write access, are forbidden (`http://aspn.activestate.com/ASPN/docs/PHP/features.safe-mode.html`).

If safe mode is switched on, no files can be uploaded and file uploads are necessary for the gallery. Therefore, you can simply specify your FTP access instructions here and PHP then uses the built-in FTP functionality for uploading pictures.

Accessibility

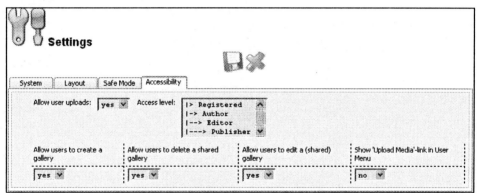

Figure 5.34: Access Rights

Here you select the default access rights by choosing yes or no in the following fields:

- Allow users to create a gallery
- Allow users to delete a published gallery
- Allow users to modify a published gallery
- Show the upload link in the user menu

Move Media

Here you can move pictures from one gallery into another in three steps:

1. Select the gallery in which the picture that you want to move is located. You receive a form displaying pictures in this gallery with a check box adjacent to each picture's filename.
2. Select the pictures to be moved by marking the appropriate check boxes.
3. Select the target gallery.

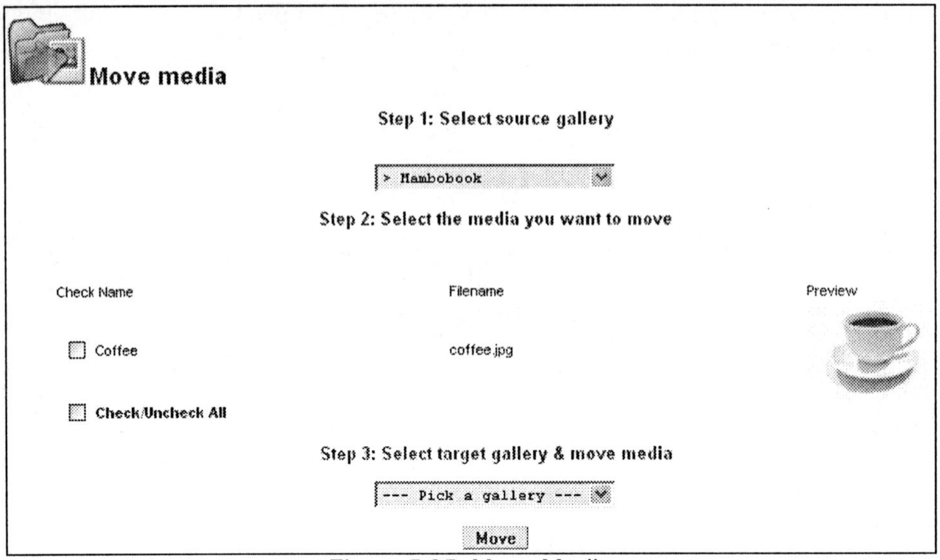

Figure 5.35: Move Media

Optimize Tables

This cleans the database tables used by the gallery. Occasionally such housekeeping may be necessary, for example, when users upload files and interrupt the process before it is finished. This creates entries in the database, although the matching pictures never got there.

Update Zoom Media Gallery

This link leads to Mike de Boer's website from where you can install the latest updates for the gallery.

Integration of the Gallery into your Website

Now you have to merge the gallery with the main menu so that it is displayed on your website. Click Menu | Main menu and then New. Select Component in the subsequent dialog and click Next (see Figure 5.7).

Give a new name to the menu entry (picture gallery) and select Zoom Media Gallery Admin in the component list. Leave the access on Public and click Save.

If you exit your web page and reload it, a new entry (picture gallery) is located in your main menu at the bottom of the page. Clicking on it will start your new component.

Depending on your choice of settings, you will see your photo galleries with a preview of the pictures. Click on the gallery link to see the previews for all pictures. If you click on a preview picture, a new page with the original picture and the information you entered is opened. Below the picture, there is a space for comments.

5.3.5 User Frontend

Depending on the access rights set, you may create galleries and upload files. A similar interface to the one described in Section 5.3.4, is at your disposal. You get to this interface via the user system link.

Lightbox

Lightbox is a personal selection of pictures displayed when you click the Lightbox icon. You can insert individual pictures and whole galleries into the Lightbox. You can find the Lightbox icon above the picture.

E-Cards

You can send pictures and a message as an e-card to a friend's e-mail address by clicking the link to your card in the e-mail. You can specify the expiry date of the e-card in the administration settings.

5.3.6 Modules for the Zoom Media Gallery

There are various modules for your gallery. For example, to show random pictures, the last five, the most visited, those with the most comments, and even a scrolling module that lets you scroll random pictures. Look around Mike de Boer's site and try out a few modules.

5.4 Comments

If you prefer interactive websites and are interested in your visitors' opinions, it would be great for your users to be able to comment on Content Items. This is possible with Arthur Konze's **AkoComment** component.

5.4.1 Installation

Download the com_akocomment20.zip file and install it using the component installer:

Figure 5.36: Installation of the AkoComment Component

Subsequently, download the cb_akocommentbot.zip file and install it using the Mambot installer:

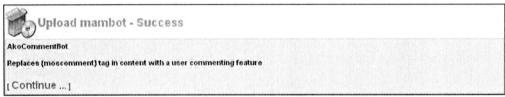

Figure 5.37: Installation of the AkoComment Mambot

At the time of writing this book, the component did not function perfectly with Mambo 4.5.2. You have to delete line 37 in the [mambo]/administrator/components/com_ akocomment/toolbar.akocomment.php file.

```
line 36 default:
line 37 //MENU_Default::MENU_Default();
line 38 break;
```

5.4.2 Administration

There are three menu entries in the menu Components | AkoComment:

View Comments

Here you can edit comments that have been posted by users. Since at this moment there are no comments present, this area is still empty.

Edit Settings

Here you can specify settings in four different tabs.

General

Main Operating Mode: Here you can decide whether comments should always be displayed or if only the Mambot command {moscomment} should be contained in the content.

Sections available: With automatic display, you can select which group of content elements automatically gets comment windows.

Autopublish Comments: Here you can specify whether comments are approved automatically and thus appear immediately on the page.

Anonymous Comments: Whether or not to allow anonymous comments.

Comment Window: Here you can choose if the comment window should appear in the same or in its own window.

Layout

Comments Sorting: Should the oldest or the most recent comment be shown first?

Form Position: Should the form be positioned below or above the comments?

Posting

BB Code Support: Should BBCode for simple formatting be supported?

Picture Support: Should pictures be permitted as part of the comments?

Smiley Support: Should smileys be displayed?

Notification

Notify Admin: Specify if an e-mail should be sent to an admin when a new comment is posted.

Admin's Email: The e-mail address of the user to which the admin message is sent.

Edit Language

Here you get a text area field for the modification of text.

5.4.3 Frontend

When you go to your website, you will see a comment window under the content elements that corresponds to your settings.

Here your visitors can post comments about your content to their heart's desire:

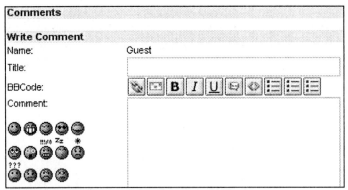

Figure 5.38: Comment Window

5.5 Multilingualism with Mambelfish

The **Mambelfish** component makes it possible to produce a multilingual website. This topic is quite complex, and using this component is not easy. In Europe, there is a demand for multilingual websites. Creating a real multilingual site with Mambo is not yet possible. You can select from many front-end language files, but the website has only one language. With Alex Kempkens' ingenious component, it is now possible to produce real multilingual websites.

The language aspect is always difficult. A web page consists of standard sentences, which are translated into language files. These language files are also used in Mambelfish. Furthermore, a standard language is specified in Global Configuration. According to requirements, users can select several target languages.

But what happens to the content?

Here, Mambelfish takes the rocky but logical route of translating all dynamic content in the translation manager into an appropriate target language. They include the menu descriptions and different categories. The content is not translated automatically; instead, you have to produce every content element in the target language.

This has the following advantages:

- Every part of your website is available in all languages.
- The user can see the entire website in a different language by a click of the mouse.

5.5.1 Installation of Mambelfish (Component and Module)

Download the mambelfish_1.5.zip file and install it from the menu option Installers | Components. After installation, you will see a message indicating that the component has been installed.

In addition, you will see an extensive greeting text. We will return to that later. For immediate results, install the appropriate module. Download the `mbf_module.zip` file and install it from the menu option Installers | Modules. After installation completes, you will see a message announcing that the module was successfully installed.

Click Modules | Site Modules and activate the module. If you look at the bottom left hand corner of your web page, you will see an empty box with the heading Mambelfish. This happens because you have not yet configured the component.

5.5.2 Mambelfish Configuration

After installing Mamblefish, install all languages that you want to offer from the Site | Languages | Install menu.

To make the languages available for Mambelfish, you have to enter the appropriate values in Components | Mambelfish | Configuration. The dialog has two tabs: Languages and Frontend.

Languages

This tab displays all the installed languages. You can select all languages and overwrite the default descriptions. In addition, you can specify the correct character set (ISO) and an image file to be displayed in place of the name, for example, a flag. You can also specify the order that languages should be displayed in the module:

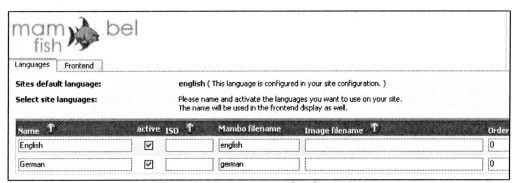

Figure 5.39: Language Configuration

Now on the web page, the module offers both languages:

Figure 5.40: Language
Selection

If you click on the language links, you will notice some differences. The most common one is the notice:

Sorry this content is not available in your selected language

Since we are working with Mambo sample data, they must be translated. Now let's look at the second tab.

Frontend

The settings for the website are defined in the following figure:

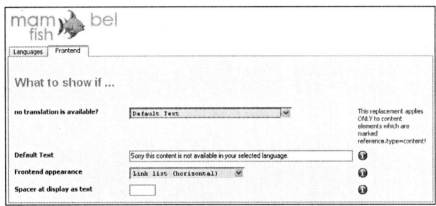

Figure 5.41: Language Configuration in Frontend

Two things need to be addressed here. First, what should happen to the display of content elements if no translation is available, and second, how should language entries in the module be displayed. For elements that have not been translated, there is an option to display alternate text. This alternate text can be chosen in the next field presented to you. The second option is to display the original text. The third option also offers the original text, however, with additional information.

The front-end layout takes place either horizontally or vertically and either as text or as an image. A separator can be entered in the field below it, for use with horizontal layout. By default, it is the pipe symbol (|).

5.5.3 Translation with Mambelfish

It is very easy to translate a web page using Mambelfish component. From the Components | Mambelfish |Translation menu, you come to the translation area of the component. You get an empty window when you first access this area. Select No translation as language and Categories as content elements. All categories, Mambobook as well as others, are now displayed. Now select the language. The display without translation changes accordingly.

Figure 5.42: Mambelfish without Translation

Click on the Mambobook link. You will get an edit form as shown in Figure 5.43:

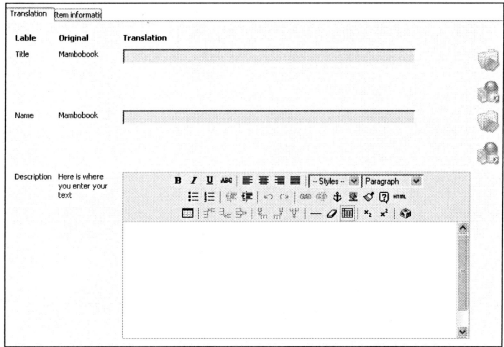

Figure 5.43: Mambelfish with Translation

If you enable the WYSIWYG editor, pasting by mouse-click may not work. If this is the case, use the *Shift + Insert* or *Ctrl + V* key combination.

Click Save to translate the first part of your website. The date of the translation appears in the categories list. Publish the category by clicking on the red cross icon.

Select English as the language in the Language field and repeat the process.

If you select All languages in the option list, translations are visible:

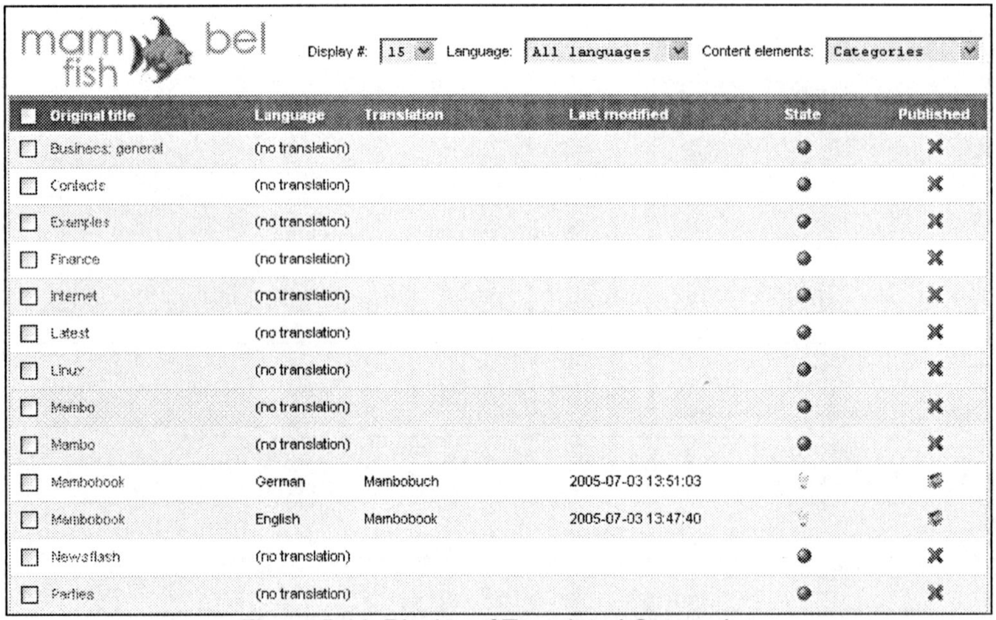

Figure 5.44: Display of Translated Categories

Repeat the process with a Content item. The fourth chapter is used as an example:

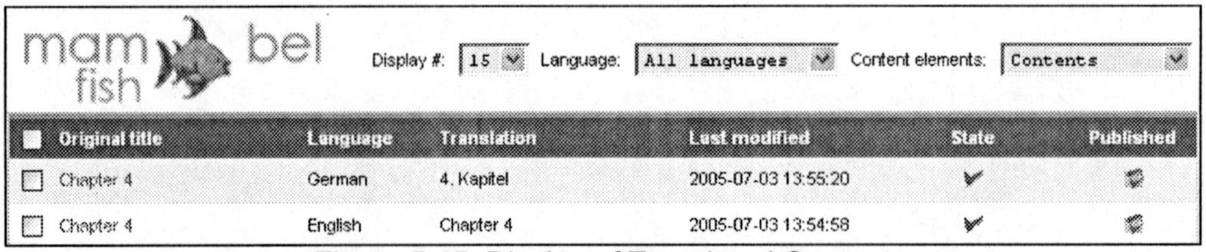

Figure 5.45: Display of Translated Content

On your website, the text appears in the language you selected. You can translate your entire website using this method. It is a lot of work but the result, especially for a business application, is respectable and competent.

5.5.4 Mambot for Mambelfish

Mambelfish Mambot can browse the translated pages using the search module.

Download the `mbf_searchbot.zip` file and click Installers | Mambots in the menu bar. Select the file and click Upload File & Install. The list of installed Mambots displays multilingual content searchbot.

Click Mambots | Site Mambots in the menu bar and publish the newly installed multilingual content searchbot. When you enter text in the search field on your website, the translated elements are scanned and displayed in the result list if a match is found.

5.5.5 Integrate your Own Components into Mambelfish

By copying a table description in XML format into the directory `[mambo]/administrator/components/com_mambelfish/contentelements/`, you can merge all components into the Mambelfish system. You can find an XML file for the sample components (see Chapter 6) in Listing 5.1 given below.

Based on this description, Mambelfish integrates the data that has to be translated into the administration interface. Mambelfish can be controlled by assigning the value 0 or 1 to the attribute `translate`.

Listing 5.1: `mambobook.xml`

```xml
<?xml version="1.0" ?>
<mambelfish type="contentelement">
  <name>Mambobook</name>
  <author>Hagen Graf</author>
  <version>1.0</version>
  <description>example from the Mambobook</description>
  <reference type="Mambobook">
    <table name="mambo_book">
     <field type="referenceid" name="id" translate="0">ID</field>
     <field type="titletext" name="text" translate="1">Text</field>
    </table>
  </reference>
</mambelfish>
```

5.6 Online Shop

E-commerce systems are always in demand and Mambo has something to offer here. The phpShop component (`http://www.mambo-phpshop.net/`) offers a complete shop system for your Mambo installation. You can find shop examples and necessary downloads on their website.

As you already know how to install the component, only a few features are listed here:

- Unlimited products and categories
- Unlimited nesting depth

- User-defined ordering
- Sale of downloadable products, such as MP3s, videos, and software
- Additional attributes of products (for example, size and color)
- Ability of auction pricing
- Import ability from CSV files
- A welcome form displays current statistics, for example, the number of customers and orders
- Administration from the Internet
- Different currencies and countries
- Different shipping addresses for customers
- Different tax rates
- SSL encryption
- Various payment options (for example, credit cards and PayPal)

5.7 Document Management

Document management is the domain of the DOCMan component (`http://www.mambodocman.com/`). With it, you can manage various kinds of documents (files) and make them available for download.

Because of its ability to create categories, you can offer a different download area for different user groups.

DOCMan is also suitable for closed work groups with the relevant documents made available in a central place.

5.8 Web Accessibility with Mambo

A website can contain elements that are difficult to understand by users with disabilities. Few content management systems provide web accessibility and Mambo is one of them.

5.8.1 xMambo

The xMambo project (`http://mambofrog.com/`) tries to make Mambo web pages usable to people with disabilities. xMambo 4.5 is a version of Mambo 4.5 Stable, which was completely rewritten to generate pure XHTML and CSS web pages and is fully compliant with section 508/WAI-Code (`http://intetics.com/faq.html`). These standards have to be satisfied, so that a website can fulfill the conditions for web accessibility.

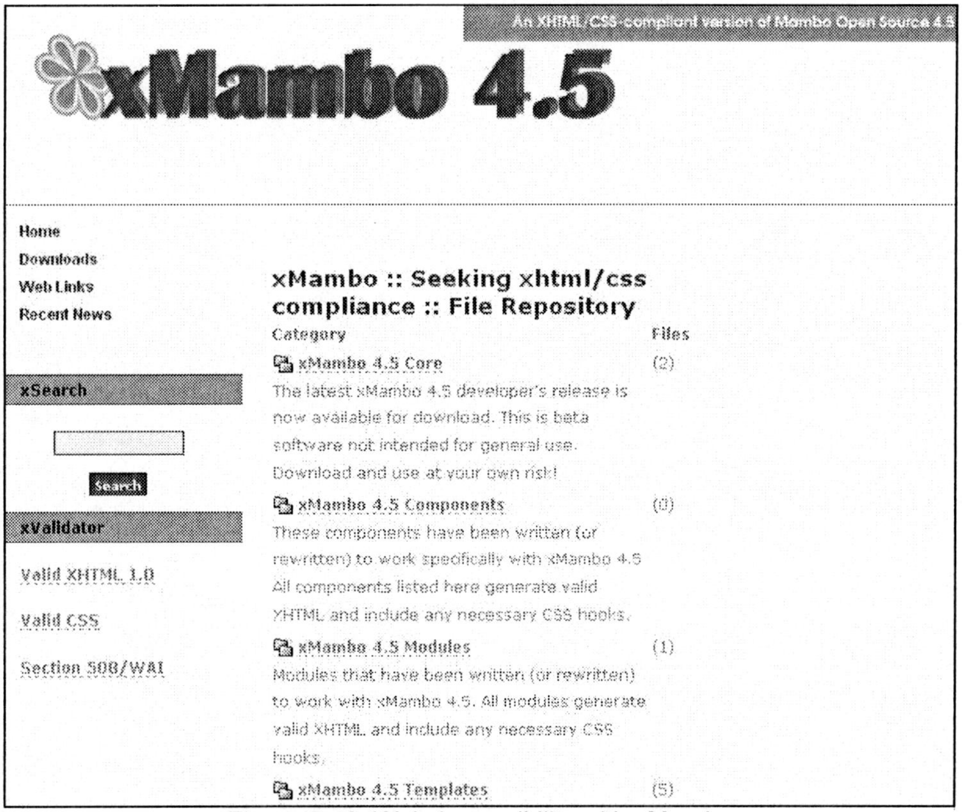

Figure 5.46: Web Accessibility with xMambo

Project xMambo now is no longer in development. However, the developers have been recruited for further Mambo development and will ensure that accessibility functions are built into Mambo version 5 out of the box.

6

Corporate Identity

Corporate Identity (CI) refers to the self-image and the appearance of an enterprise. This appearance, the identity, either results from the enterprise's tradition or it is completely invented in a newly created establishment. This identity is important to give the customer a feel for the enterprise and to enable recognition.

Corporate Identity includes:

- Corporate Image (price, product, and advertising strategy)
- Corporate Design (visual appearance)
- Corporate Communication
- Corporate Behavior (behavior of coworkers with each other and to the outside world)

These areas need to be considered while developing a website. In this chapter, we will examine Corporate Design. At a minimum, it consists of a logo, a character font, and the house colors that the enterprise uses.

The visitors to your website should recognize your enterprise on the first visit.

6.1 HTML/XHTML, CSS, and XML

The abbreviations HTML/XHTML, CSS, and XML stand for Internet technologies that Mambo works with. The World Wide Web Consortium (http://www.w3.org/) standardizes these technologies.

6.1.1 HTML/XHTML

The World Wide Web is based on HTML, a page-description language. It is not a programming language, but a text-description language.

Every text consists of structures like headings, lists, bold and italic areas, tables, and much more. HTML works with so-called **tags**. A tag has an opening and a closing form. For example, a first-level heading looks like this:

```
<h1>This is a heading</h1>
```

The tags are interpreted in a browser and the text is displayed according to their meaning.

HTML is easy to learn and a tutorial can be found at `http://www.w3schools.com/html/`. HTML is not developed any further and the successor to HTML is XHTML version 1.0.

6.1.2 CSS

Cascading Style Sheets (CSS) are an extension to HTML. CSS is not a programming language, but a vocabulary for defining the format properties of HTML elements.

With the help of CSS commands, you can determine that first-level headings should have a character size of 18 points in the character font Arial, are not bold, and have a spacing of 1.9 cm to the next paragraph.

Such options are not possible with pure HTML and were not necessary while developing it. With the progressive commercialization of the Internet, additional formatting possibilities do become more important.

CSS data can be included in HTML in the following three ways:

In the Central HTML File
The CSS commands are defined in the head section of the HTML file:

```
<head>
<title>title of the file</title>
<style type="text/css">
<!--
/* ... this is where the CSS commands are defined ... */
-->
</style>
</head>
```

In a Separate CSS File
If the CSS commands apply to several HTML files, they can be stored in a separate file and the path to this file can be specified in the HTML head section. This is the version that Mambo uses:

```
<head>
<title>title of the file</title>
<link rel="stylesheet" type="text/css" href="formate.css">
</head>
```

Within an HTML Tag

CSS commands can be integrated within an HTML tag:

```
<body>
<h1 style="… CSS command ...">...</h1>
</body>
```

Combinations

These three methods can be combined without any problem in an HTML file. It is, for instance, possible to overwrite CSS commands in a central HTML file that applies to all pages with the subsequent source code of an HTML page. It is better to use the central file because overriding it results in unclear structures.

6.1.3 XML

The **Extensible Markup Language (XML)** is a universe in itself. It represents a metalanguage in which other languages are formulated. To a certain extent, it is the mother of all languages. For our purposes, you need XML as the description language for the metadata of the templates that you want to create. These metadata are primarily important for the template installer and the display in the Template Manager. In principle, these data consist of opening and closing tags. For example:

```
<name>Mambo book</name>
```

One difference between HTML and XML is that in XML no tags are predefined. For this reason, one is free in the organization of the structures and naming of tags.

6.2 Create Your Own Templates

Now we want to create our own template. There are several things to consider before we have a finished template package.

6.2.1 Concept

Before you start working, you have to create a concept. The work starts with a sketch or a diagram, especially when producing templates. Whether you create this sketch with programs like Adobe Photoshop (`http://www.adobe.com/products/photoshop/`), Microsoft Paint, which comes with Windows, the open-source program Gimp (`http://www.gimp.org/`), or with a piece of paper and markers is up to you.

Fixed Size or Variable

You can create two kinds of templates: templates that adapt their structure to the size of the browser window and templates that have a fixed size. An example for the first flexible layout is if you have 2048 pixels on your screen and the browser window is maximized, then your page is stretched accordingly. It can look strange if you use graphics and non-scalable elements like logos and signatures in your template. You have no control of what it is going to look like.

The other variation is to decide on a certain resolution and to position all elements exactly on the pixels in the template. The advantage is that your webpage always looks the way you want. Unfortunately, you do not know the default screen resolution of your page. Your page fills the screen with a resolution of 800 x 600 pixels. On a large screen with 1400 x 1050 pixels, it occupies about a quarter of the screen surface and looks a little lost.

There is no real solution for this dilemma. You have to weigh the pros and cons and make a decision.

If you prefer the fixed size, you should select a size that looks presentable on most screens, which are 800 x 600 pixels. Since the browser has a scroll bar on the right side and the browser window is framed, the available width is even smaller, so you have a maximum of 780 pixels to work with.

Structure

You are dealing with structured data and first have to determine a general allocation. Mambo normally uses a structure shown in the following figure:

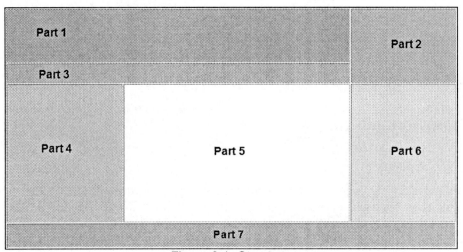

Figure 6.1: Structure

Section 1:

- Part 1: This is where your logo or a picture and the page name go.
- Part 2: This is where the search field is.
- Part 3: Here is the linked navigation path (Breadcrumbs).

Section 2:

- Part 4: The most important menus are shown in the left column.
- Part 5: The actual page content goes here.
- Part 6: The right column is a place for additional menus.

Section 3:

- Part 7: The bottom part is the footer.

6.2.2 HTML Conversion

Now you have to convert the concept into HTML. Depending on the program with which you created it, there is a possibility that the picture can be automatically converted to HTML code. You can also do the conversion manually in a text editor, in an HTML editor like Macromedia Dreamweaver (http://www.macromedia.com/software /dreamweaver/), or in one of the numerous free HTML editors (http://www. thefreecountry.com/webmaster/htmleditors.shtml).

The source code of the HTML conversion looks like Listing 6.1. The code is kept simple and does not correspond to the XHTML standard in the head section.

Listing 6.1: HTML Basic Structure

```
<html>
<head>
<title>Untitled Document</title>
</head>
<body bgcolor="#FFFFFF" text="#000000">
<table width="780" border="1">
<!-- Part 1 -->
<tr>
    <!-- Area 1 -->
    <td colspan="2" height="89" bgcolor="#F5C228"> </td>
    <!-- Area 2 -->
    <td width="178" height="120" rowspan="2" bgcolor="#FFCC33">  
                                                                </td>
</tr>
<tr>
    <!-- Area 3 -->
    <td colspan="2" height="33" bgcolor="#FFCC33"> </td>
</tr>
<!-- Part 2 -->
<tr>
    <!-- Area 4 -->
    <td width="197" height="233" bgcolor="#F5EE28">   </td>
    <!-- Area 5 -->
    <td width="389" height="233"> </td>
    <!-- Area 6 -->
    <td width="178" height="233" bgcolor="#FFFF33">   </td>
</tr>
<!-- Part 3 -->
<tr bgcolor="#FFCC33">
    <!-- Area 7 -->
```

```
        <td colspan="3" height="40"> </td>
    </tr>
</table>
</body>
</html>
```

If you open this source code in a browser, the structure looks similar to our concept (see Figure 6.1). You must store this source code in a file named index.php.

Figure 6.2: Basic Structure of HTML

To see the division better, the table is drawn with a border (attribute border="1"). Here you can give your creative juices free reign when it comes to colors and logos.

6.2.3 File Structure of the Template

Now it's time to think about certain conventions. The template has to be stored in a special directory structure. If required, you can work directly with your local Mambo installation. If that is too unclear, you can also store the template in an arbitrary place on your hard drive. You have to adhere to the following file structure:

/templates/[name of the template]/

/templates/[name of the template]/css/

/templates/[name of the template]/images/

The name of the template cannot contain blanks and other special characters. Later, the template installer has to create a directory from this name. Depending on the operating system, exotic combinations of characters can cause problems; also, the name should be meaningful. For example, if you make the 'template chooser' module available on your website, this name will be offered to your visitors in the selection list. I am using mambobook as my template.

Various files with certain names have to be present in the template directories. Besides the image files of your template, all other file names have to agree with the defaults.

/templates/mambobook/index.php

This is the basic version of the HTML file that we created earlier. It has to have the .php ending, since the dynamic Mambo module element, which we will insert later, has to be interpreted by PHP.

/templates/mambobook/template_thumbnail.png

A preview picture of your template for selection in Mambo administration and in the template chooser module will be available. Preview pictures have a format of approximately 227 x 162 pixels.

/templates/mambobook/templateDetails.xml

This file represents the construction manual for the 'template installer'. Here you specify the location where the files are to be copied. For the example template, you can use the file from Listing 6.2 and provide your own data.

Listing 6.2: templateDetails.xml

```
<?xml version="1.0" encoding="iso-8859-1"?>
<mosinstall type="template" version="4.5.2">
<name>mambobook</name>
<creationDate>03/23/05</creationDate>
<author>Hagen Graf</author>
<copyright>GNU/GPL</copyright>
<authorEmail>hagen_39393@yahoo.de</authorEmail>
<authorUrl>http://www.alternative-unternehmensberatung.de</authorUrl>
<version>0.01</version>
<description>This is the first attempt at a template</description>
<files>
<filename>index.php</filename>
<filename>template_thumbnail.png</filename>
</files>
<images>
<filename>images/logo.png</filename>
</images>
<css>
<filename>css/template_css.css</filename>
</css>
</mosinstall>
```

/templates/mambobook/css/template_css.css

This is the CSS file of your template and the organization of the CSS file is open to you. However, there are standard descriptions for various side elements. You can find a table of these elements in the Appendix. For your first attempt, you need an empty CSS file with this name.

/templates/mambobook/images/[user-defined picture files]

Here you can store arbitrary image files, which will be used in your template. The installer then copies the files into the 'image' sorter.

6.2.4 First Trial Run

You can see and access your new template in Mambo administration once you have reconstructed all the structures in the [mambo]/templates/ subdirectory:

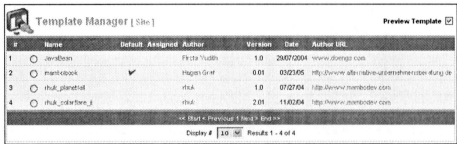

Figure 6.3: New Template

When you open your website, you will see the structure as shown in Figure 6.2. Unfortunately, no content is shown yet. Since this content is produced dynamically, you have to integrate it piece by piece into your new template.

6.2.5 Integration of the Mambo Module

The integration of the Mambo module takes place by means of PHP commands that are embedded into the HTML code. If you insert the following lines in place of the title tag in the head section of the index.php file, the favicon and the title of the page are displayed:

```
<head>
<?php mosShowHead(); ?>
</head>
```

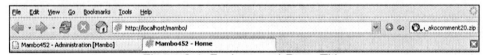

Figure 6.4: Favicon and Page Title

If you view the source code of this page, you will notice that Mambo has written the entire metadata, which you had entered in Administration, into the HTML code.

Listing 6.3: Mambo Metadata

```
...
<head>
<title>Mambo452 - Home</title>
<meta name="description" content="Mambo - the dynamic portal engine
and content management system" />
<meta name="keywords" content="mambo, Mambo" />
<meta name="Generator" content="Mambo - Copyright 2000 - 2005 Miro
International Pty Ltd. All rights reserved." />
<meta name="robots" content="index, follow" />
```

```
<link rel="alternate" type="application/rss+xml" title="Mambobook
Test RSS"
href="http://localhost/mambo/cache/rss20.xml" />
<link rel="shortcut icon"
href="http://localhost/mambo/images/favicon.ico" />
</head>
...
```

Since this has worked so well, we will waste no time and get to the other relevant PHP modules that deal with functions. For example, the function mosLoad-Modules() expects the location of the module (right, left, user1...) as parameter. You can assign this place in the 'Module Manager'. The function then displays all modules with the appropriate parameter.

The following listing shows the complete source code of the index.php file with PHP modules:

Listing 6.4: index.php with Mambo Modules

```
<html><head>
<?php mosShowHead(); ?>
</head>
<body bgcolor="#FFFFFF" text="#000000">
<table width="780" border="1">
  <!-- Part 1 -->
  <tr>
    <!-- Area 1 -->
    <td colspan="2" height="89" bgcolor="#F5C228"> </td>
    <!-- Area 2 -->
    <td width="178" height="120" rowspan="2" bgcolor="#FFCC33">
    <?php mosLoadModules ( 'user4' ); ?>
    </td>
  </tr>
  <tr>
    <!-- Area 3 -->
    <td colspan="2" height="33" bgcolor="#FFCC33">
    <?php mosPathWay(); ?>
    </td>
  </tr>
  <!-- Part 2 -->
  <tr>
    <!-- Area 4 -->
    <td width="197" height="233" bgcolor="#F5EE28" valign="top">
    <?php mosLoadModules ( 'left' ); ?>
    </td>
    <!-- Area 5 -->
    <td width="389" height="233" valign="top">
    <?php mosMainBody(); ?>
    </td>
    <!-- Area 6 -->
    <td width="178" height="233" bgcolor="#FFFF33" valign="top">
    <?php mosLoadModules ( 'right' ); ?>
    </td>
  </tr>
  <!-- Part 3 -->
  <tr bgcolor="#FFCC33">
    <!-- Area 7 -->
    <td colspan="3" height="40">
```

```
<?php include_once( $GLOBALS['mosConfig_absolute_path']
'/includes/footer.php'); ?>
</td>
</tr>
</table></body></html>
```

If you open the homepage with the changed HTML code on a local server, you will see dynamic content. Your new template is filled with data. You are now working with pure HTML code and the results look like they could benefit from some visual improvement:

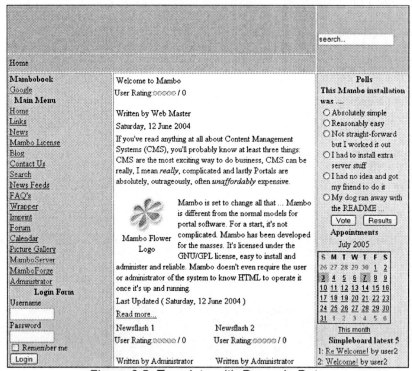

Figure 6.5: Template with Dynamic Data

To refine the visual aspect, we will take a small step into CSS formatting. Copy the following code into your `template_css.css` file (Listing 6.5). Here it is specified that the default font is Arial, the links are not to be underlined, and the script will be displayed in another color and bold font if you roll over a link with your mouse (see http://en.selfhtml.org/css/).

Listing 6.5: template_css.css

```
body {
font-family: Arial, Helvetica, Sans Serif;
}
a:link, a:visited {
color: #ff6600;
text-decoration: none;
```

```
font-weight: bold;
}
a:hover {
color: #C43C03;
text-decoration: none;
font-weight: bold;
}
```

Now your template looks a little more attractive. Point the mouse on the Search link in the main menu. The link is displayed in bold and in another color:

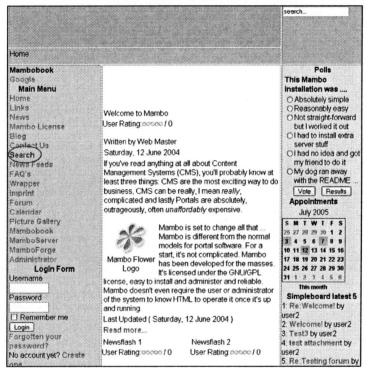

Figure 6.6: Template with CSS file

6.2.6 Creating a Template Package

To complete your template, create a current preview picture of your template (template_ thumbnail.png) and pack all the files with subdirectories into a ZIP archive.

In addition, assign all files and folders to the folder [mambo]/templates/mambobook/ and pack all the contents into the mambobook.zip file. Make a backup of this file and the ZIP file.

To test the installation, remove the template from the Template Manager. To accomplish this, specify another template as the default (select the template and click Publish), delete the newly created template by selecting it, and click Delete.

6.2.7 Installation with the Mambo Template Installer

After you have eliminated traces of development, go to the menu Installers | Template Site, select the mambobook.zip file, and click Upload File & Install. You will see the success screen of the template installer. A description from the XML file is displayed in the following figure:

Figure 6.7: Uploading the New Template

If you click Continue, the newly created template is displayed in the Template Manager with a preview picture:

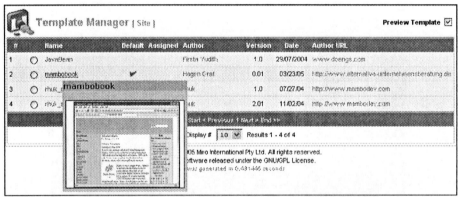

Figure 6.8: New Template in the Template Manager

6.3 Dreamweaver Extension

There is an extension for the HTML editor Dreamweaver with which you can produce templates. After installing the extension, you get a Mambo pallet with the available elements, which you can insert with a mouse-click into your template (http://www.mambosolutions.com/dw_tutorial/).

7

Your Own Program Extensions

Let's say that you want to solve a problem for which there is no completed Mambo component, for example, a list of your used cars or your addresses. Simply extend the functional range with new components, modules, and Mambots. What looks complicated at first sight is feasible with basic knowledge of PHP.

After your experience with building templates, you know what is to come. To get an idea of what is being discussed here, you need:

- A new component consisting of a frontend, a Mambo administration, and a special table in the database
- An additional module to display the entries on your website
- A search Mambot to browse your new content

Here is an example of a simple list on the website:

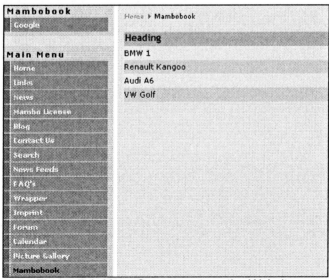

Figure 7.1: Your Component on the Website

This list can have user-defined content (addresses, offers, etc.). For the customer, it is usually sufficient to see the list. The administrator, however, has to administer the list by:

- Making new entries
- Modifying existing entries
- Deleting existing entries

To make the example simple, we are displaying and working on only one field. This way the principle becomes clear and the example can be easily extended into multiple fields. The following figure illustrates the basic administrative interface of the list:

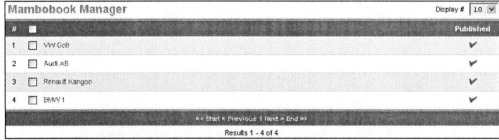

Figure 7.2: Your Component in Mambo Administration

7.1 Sample Mambobook Component

Let's start with the component. Since this component can become the basis for many different lists, I call it Mambobook. You can download the finished example, install it like the other components, and reproduce it manually. The advantage of reproduction is that you can gradually check out the structures and get a taste for it.

7.1.1 The MySQL Table

Since you are starting from scratch, you need a new table in MySQL. You can create the desired table in the following ways:

- Write a PHP program that creates the table
- Work from the MySQL console
- Control MySQL with a tool like phpMyAdmin

With xampplite and most web space providers, you receive the phpMyAdmin tool for database management (http://www.phpmyadmin.net/). With this program, which is written in PHP like Mambo, you can directly manipulate your MySQL tables. Activate phpMyAdmin in xampplite by opening the http://localhost/phpmyadmin URL in your browser:

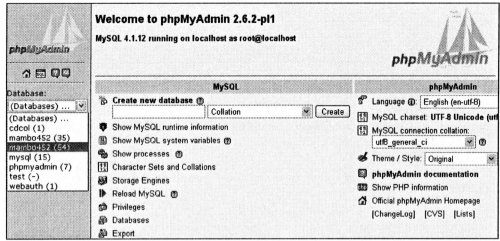

Figure 7.3: phpMyAdmin

From the left panel, select the database that contains your Mambo tables. If you have only one database in your hosting packet, you end up directly in your Mambo database with some providers by opening phpMyAdmin. With xampplite, you can set up numerous databases if required.

Databases like MySQL are controlled with SQL commands. The **Structured Query Language** is a data manipulation language that is similar to set theory, which emerged in the seventies. The idea behind SQL is to use a few commands like `Alter`, `Delete`, `Insert`, and `Create` with a precisely defined quantity of data.

For the component example, you need SQL commands to create a table and insert data.

Listing 7.1: SQL Commands for the Example Table

```sql
-- Table structure for table `mos_mambo_book`
CREATE TABLE `mos_mambo_book` (
        `id` INT NOT NULL AUTO_INCREMENT,
        `text` TEXT NOT NULL,
        `published` TINYINT(1) NOT NULL,
        PRIMARY KEY (`id`) );
-- Data for table `mos_mambo_book`
INSERT INTO `mos_mambo_book` VALUES (11,'BMW 1', 1);
INSERT INTO `mos_mambo_book` VALUES (9,'Renault Kangoo', 1);
INSERT INTO `mos_mambo_book` VALUES (8,'Audi A6', 1);
INSERT INTO `mos_mambo_book` VALUES (7,'VW Golf', 1);
INSERT INTO `mos_mambo_book` VALUES (10,'Mercedes G', 1);
```

To deliver these SQL commands to the database, click SQL, insert the commands into the form, and click OK:

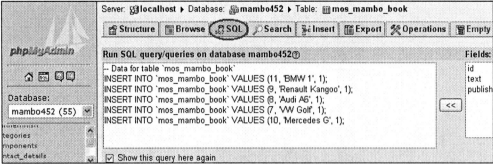

Figure 7.4: Importing the Table Structure

MySQL creates the new mos_mambo_book table and inserts five data records. Click mos_mambo_book and then Show to see the following result:

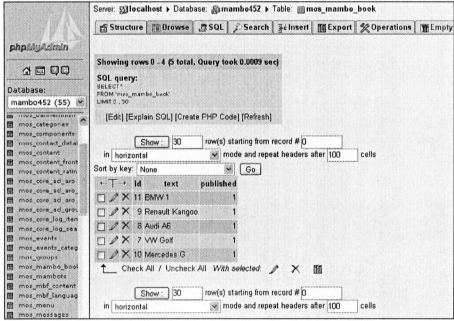

Figure 7.5: Newly Created mos_mambo_book Table

With this, we have created the table and can leave phpMyAdmin for now. The installer component will later assume this job with the automatic installation in Mambo.

7.1.2 The Frontend

Your homepage is the frontend. To increase the anticipation a little bit, we will start with the frontend.

If you take a quick look into your [mambo]/components directory, you will notice that all directories begin with com_ followed by a description (com_contact, com_content, etc.). This is where your installed components are stored. To open a component in the browser, specify the name of this subdirectory as value in the option parameter in the URL:

```
http://localhost/mambo/index.php?option=com_contact
```

For your components, create a new subdirectory with the name [mambo]/components/ mambobook. Create two files in this subdirectory:

- mambobook.php: This file contains the logic in pure PHP code. For example, the database is queried here.

- mambobook.html.php: This file contains the presentation of the data. PHP is also used here, but the emphasis lies on HTML and CSS code.

mambobook.php
This file consists of four arrays and a few more lines (see Listing 7.2).

The first array ensures that it is not possible to open the file directly by the input of the file name and it can be opened only from another file. This is a security measure because the component is not executable without the Mambo system. Moreover, the source code of the second (mambo.html.php) file is merged here. Since this merging is standard for the HTML interface, there is a getPath() procedure that looks in the same directory for an appropriate file to merge with. The name is created from the directory's name with an html.php ending.

In the second array, parameters are transferred. Here the HTML title of the page appears in the upper blue bar of the browser.

The third array contains a case differentiation. You can open the component with different parameters and interpret them here. For example, the differentiation here could be between an overview and an individual view.

The fourth array contains the actual logic. Here the database is queried, a result array is created, and the showtable() procedure in the HTML_mambobook class is opened. This class is in the merged mambobook.html.php file.

Listing 7.2: mambobook.php

```php
<?php
//Array 1
/* ensure that this file is called up by another file */
defined( '_VALID_MOS' ) or ( 'Direct access of this file is
prohibited.'
);
// Loading of the HTML class
require_once( $mainframe->getPath( 'front_html' ) );
// Array 2
$mainframe->setPageTitle( "Example component Mambobook" );
// Array 3
switch( $task ) {
```

```
    case 'free':
      // more display possibilities
      break;
    default:
      listMambobook();
      break;
  }
  // Array 4
  function listMambobook( ) {
    global $database;
    /* SQL query of all published entries */
    $query = "SELECT * FROM #__mambo_book WHERE published='1'";
    $database->setQuery( $query );
    $rows = $database->loadObjectList();
    HTML_mambobook::showtable( &$rows );
  }
  ?>
```

mambobook.html.php

The mambobook.html.php file (see Listing 7.3) contains the HTML_mambobook class. A class is like a structural plan with many procedures. Our small class contains only the showTable procedure.

An array is handed over to the showTable procedure (&$rows) and is represented in a table. To achieve this, a foreach loop continues running until there are no more elements.

With each run a different value is generated for the variable $k. $k controls the CSS class of a table row (class="sectiontableentry<?php echo ($k+1); ?>"). Consequently, the rows are reproduced in two different colors as illustrated in Figure 7.1.

In principle, as many procedures as desired can be implemented in the class; beside the table view there could also be, for example, an individual view.

The class represents a structural design and should be filled with data. This makes it comparable to a template. For this reason, the class is also merged with the mambobook.php file and is started by running HTML_mambobook::showtable($rows);.

Listing 7.3: mambobook.html.php

```
  <?php
  /* ensuring that this file is called up from another file */
  defined( '_VALID_MOS' ) or ( 'Direct access to this file is
  prohibited.'
  );
  class HTML_mambobook {
    // Procedure for building the table
    function showTable( $rows ) {
      ?>
      <table width="100%" border="0" cellspacing="0" cellpadding="0"
                                                    align="center">
      <tr>
      <td height="20" class="sectiontableheader">
      <?php echo "heading"; ?>
      </td>
      </tr>
      <?php
```

```
// the variable $k helps to enable the different colors
// per row.
$k = 0;
foreach ($rows as $row) {
  ?>
  <tr>
  // $k takes on the value 0 or 1 and thereby calls
  // either the CSS class sectiontableentry1 or
  // sectiontableentry2
  <td height="20" class="sectiontableentry<?php echo ($k+1); ?>">
  // access to the DB field text
  <?php echo $row->text; ?>
  </td>
  <?php
  $k = 1 - $k;
}
?>
</table>
<?php
  }
}
?>
```

7.1.3 Integration into the Main Menu

Mambo cannot detect the component since it is not completely installed. However, you can open it via the URL http://localhost/mambo/index.php?option=com_mambobook.

You can merge the components with the main menu at this stage of development via the Link-URL option. In Mambo administration, click Menu | Main menu | New. At the bottom right, select Link-URL and click Next. Here you can enter a description and the above-mentioned link:

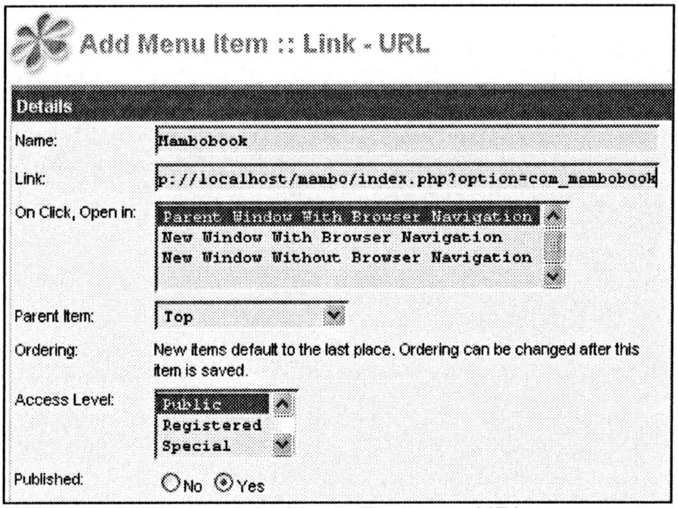

Figure 7.6: Menu Entry per URL

If you open your website, you should see the menu link Mambobook. Click on it to view the table shown in Figure 7.1.

That was surprisingly simple, wasn't it? You should seriously try to become familiar with object-oriented programming and the syntaxes of PHP, HTML, and CSS. Nevertheless, you can still create impressive tables with a few lines of code.

7.1.4 Mambo Administration

Displaying data on the webpage was relatively simple, but administering data, naturally, will be a little more complex. Here you have to display the data, modify it, reinsert it, and delete it. This implies substantially more functionality than on the webpage.

The Component Table
Mambo administers the menu entries of all components in the mos_components table. Since you are not using an installer and building everything by hand, you need two new menu entries.

Open phpMyAdmin, select the mos_components table, click SQL, insert the two SQL commands (see Listing 7.4), and click OK to confirm.

Listing 7.4: SQL Commands Menu Entry

```
INSERT INTO `mos_components` VALUES ( 'Mambobook',
'option=com_mambobook', 0, 0,
'option=com_mambobook', 'Mambobook', 'com_mambobook', 0,
'js/ThemeOffice/component.png', 0, '');
INSERT INTO `mos_components` VALUES ('Edit entries', '', 0, 46,
'option=com_mambobook&act=all', 'Edit entries', 'com_mambobook', 0,
'js/ThemeOffice/component.png', 0, '');
```

By inserting these two data sets, you extend the Components menu by a main Mambobook entry and an Edit Entries submenu entry:

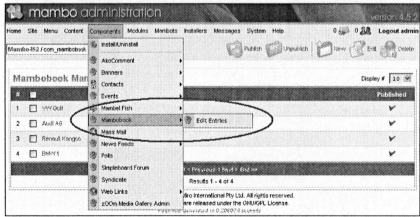

Figure 7.7: New Component in the Components Menu

In addition, you can specify what the respective menu entry calls up (option=com_ mambobook&act=all') and the picture that is to appear on the left, next to the menu ('js/ThemeOffice/component.png'). You can find the pictures in the [mambo]/includes/js/ThemeOffice folder.

This time you need, not two, but five files. Create a subdirectory called com_mambobook under the [mambo]/administration/components/ directory. In this subdirectory, create the following five files:

- admin.mambobook.php
- mambobook.class.php
- admin.mambobook.html.php
- toolbar.mambobook.html.php
- toolbar.mambobook.php

admin.mambobook.php

This file contains the logic. Here we go another step further and partially swap the database queries to mambobook.class.php. In principle, the structure is specified like the front-end logic. The file is more extensive, since several cases are possible and in each case, it must be implemented with a function. In addition, the access rights are examined at the beginning, since we are in Mambo administration.

Listing 7.5: admin.mambobook.php

```php
<?php
defined( '_VALID_MOS' ) or ( 'Direct access to this file is
prohibited.'
);
// Examine access rights
if (!($acl->acl_check( 'administration', 'edit', 'users',
$my->usertype, 'components', 'all' ) | $acl->acl_check(
'administration', 'edit', 'users', $my->usertype, 'components',
'com_newsfeeds' ))) {
mosRedirect( 'index2.php', _NOT_AUTH );
}
// Loading of the database class and the HTML class
require_once( $mainframe->getPath( 'admin_html' ) );
require_once( $mainframe->getPath( 'class' ) );
$task = mosGetParam( $_REQUEST, 'task', array(0) );
// Case differentiation
switch ($task) {
  case "publish":
    publishMambobook( $id, 1, $option );
    break;
  case "unpublish":
    publishMambobook( $id, 0, $option );
    break;
  case "new":
    editMambobook( 0, $option );
    break;
  case "edit":
    editMambobook( $id[0], $option );
```

```
            break;
        case "remove":
          removeMambobook( $id, $option );
            break;
        case "save":
          saveMambobook( $option );
            break;
        case "cancel":
          cancelMambobook( $option );
            break;
        default:
          showMambobook( $option );
            break;
    }
    // Publishing of the Entries
    function publishMambobook( $cid, $publish, $option ) {
      global $database;
      if (count( $cid ) < 1) {
        // the next row represents a if - else:
        // when $publish, then 'publish' - else 'unpublish'
        $action = $publish ? 'publish' : 'unpublish';
        echo "<script> alert('Select an item to ".$action."');
                                        window.history.go(-
1);</script>\n";
        exit;
      }
      $cids = implode( ',', $cid );
      $database->setQuery( "UPDATE #__mambo_book SET published=($publish)
                                        WHERE id IN ($cids)");
      if (!$database->query()) {
        echo "<script> alert('".$database->getErrorMsg()."');
                                        window.history.go(-1);
</script>\n";
        exit();
      }
      if (count( $cid ) == 1) {
        $row = new mosMambobook( $database );
        $row->checkin( $cid[0] );
      }
      mosRedirect( "index2.php?option=$option" );
    }
    // Create new entry (id = 0)
    // or change entry with id = n
    function editMambobook $cid, $option ) {
      global $database;
      $row = new mosMambobook( $database );
      $row->load( $cid );
      // call up the procedure editMambobook in the
      // class HTML_mambobook
      HTML_mambobook::editMambobook( $row, $option );
    }
    // Deletion of entries
    function removeMambobook( $cid, $option ) {
      global $database;
      if (!is_array( $cid ) || count( $cid ) < 1) {
        echo "<script> alert('Please select an entry to delete');
window.history.go(-1);</script>\n";
        exit;
      }
```

```
    $cids = implode( ',', $cid );
    $database->setQuery( "DELETE FROM #__mambo_book WHERE id IN
                                            ($cids)" );
    if (!$database->query()) {
      echo "<script> alert('".$database->getErrorMsg()."');
                                    window.history.go(-1);
</script>\n";
    }
    mosRedirect( "index2.php?option=$option" );
}
// save entry
function saveMambobook( $option ) {
    global $database;
    $row = new mosMambobook( $database );
    if (!$row->bind( $_POST )) {
      echo "<script> alert('".$row->getError()."');
                                window.history.go(-1);
</script>\n";
      exit();
    }
    if (!$row->store()) {
      echo "<script> alert('".$row->getError()."');
                                window.history.go(-1);
</script>\n";
      exit();
    }
    mosRedirect( "index2.php?option=$option" );
}
// abort the current action
function cancelMambobook( $option ) {
    global $database;
    $row = new mosMambobook( $database );
    $row->bind( $_POST );
    $row->checkin();
    mosRedirect( "index2.php?option=$option" );
}
// listing of the entries
function showMambobook($option) {
    global $database, $mainframe;
    $limit = $mainframe->getUserStateFromRequest( "viewlistlimit",
                                            'limit', 10 );
    $limitstart = $mainframe->getUserStateFromRequest(
                            "view{$option}limitstart",
'limitstart', 0 );
    // count entries
    $database->setQuery("SELECT count(*) FROM #__mambo_book");
    $total = $database->loadResult();
    echo $database->getErrorMsg();
    // integration of the navigation elements
    require_once("includes/pageNavigation.php");
    $pageNav = new mosPageNav( $total, $limitstart, $limit );
    $database->setQuery( "SELECT * FROM #__mambo_book ORDER BY id LIMIT
                                                $pageNav-
>limitstart,$pageNav->limit" );
    $rows = $database->loadObjectList();
    if ($database->getErrorNum()) {
      echo $database->stderr();
      return false;
    }
```

```
    HTML_mambobook::showMambobook( $rows, $pageNav, $option );
}?>
```

mambobook.class.php

Here the data set structure is swapped into its own class, derived from the mosDBTable class. mosDBTable is a class in the /includes/database.php file and makes fundamental procedures for database access available.

Listing 7.6: mambobook.class.php

```php
<?php
defined( '_VALID_MOS' ) or ( 'Direct access of this file is
prohibited.' );
// the class mosMambobook is derived from the
// existing class mosDBTable
class mosMambobook extends mosDBTable {
    // Declaration and Initialization of the instance variables
    // INT(11) AUTO_INCREMENT
    var $id=null;
    // TEXT
    var $text=null;
    // TINYINT(1)
    var $published=null;
    // the constructor is called up by the instantiation
    function mosMambobook( &$db ) {
        //invocation of the constructorof the mosDBTable class
        $this->mosDBTable( '#__mambo_book', 'id', $db );
    }
}?>
```

admin.mambobook.html.php

As described in the front-end component, the HTML_mambobook class refers to the presentation of the data. The HTML and CSS structures are created using the data from admin.mambobook.php.

Listing 7.7: admin.mambobook.html.php

```php
<?php
defined( '_VALID_MOS' ) or ( 'Direct access of this file is
prohibited.'
);
class HTML_mambobook {
    // procedure showMambobook
    // creates the index table
    function showMambobook( &$rows, $pageNav, $option ) {
        // HTML starts here, combined with short
        // PHP echo announcements for creating table
        ?>
        <form action="index2.php" method="post" name="adminForm">
        //
        <table cellpadding="4" border="0" width="100%">
        <tr>
        <td class="sectionname">Mambobook Manager</td>
        <td nowrap>Display #</td>
        <td> <?php echo $pageNav->writeLimitBox(); ?> </td>
        </tr>
        </table>
        <table cellpadding="4" border="0" width="100%" class="adminlist">
```

```
<tr>
<th width="20">#</th>
<th width="20"><input type="checkbox" name="toggle" value=""
 onclick="checkAll(<?php echo count($rows); ?>);" /></th>
<th>entries</th>
<th>Published</th>
</tr>
<?php
$k = 0;
for($i=0; $i < count( $rows ); $i++) {
   $row = $rows[$i];
   $img = $row->published ? 'tick.png' : 'publish_x.png';
   $task = $row->published ? 'unpublish' : 'publish';
   ?>
   <tr class="<?php echo "row$k"; ?>">
   <td align="center" > <?php echo $I + $pageNav->limitstart+1; ?>
                                                            </td>
   <td><input type="checkbox" id="cb<?php echo $i;?>" name="id[]"
                                              value="<?php
    echo $row->id; ?>" onclick="isChecked(this.checked);" /></td>
   <td><a href="#edit" onclick="return listItemTask('cb<?php echo
    $i;?>','edit')"><?php echo $row->text; ?></a></td>
   <td width="10%" align="center"><a href="javascript: void(0);"
                                                  onclick="return
    listItemTask('cb<?php echo $i;?>','<?php echo $task;?>')"><img
    src="images/<?php echo
$img;?>" border="0" alt="" /></a></td>
   </tr>
   <?php
   $k = 1 - $k;
}
?>
<tr>
<th align="center" colspan="10"> <?php echo $pageNav-
                                  >writePagesLinks(); ?></th>
</tr>
<tr>
<td align="center" colspan="10"> <?php echo $pageNav-
                                  >writePagesCounter();
 ?></td>
</tr>
</table>
<input type="hidden" name="option"
                     value="<?php echo $option; ?>" />
<input type="hidden" name="task" value="" />
<input type="hidden" name="boxchecked" value="0" />
</form>
<?php
}
// this procedure represents the edit mask
function editMambobook( &$row, $option ) {
  mosMakeHtmlSafe( $row, ENT_QUOTES );
  // JavaScript-Code for the examination of forms starts here
  ?>
  <script language="javascript" type="text/javascript">
    function submitbutton(pressbutton) {
    var form = document.adminForm;
    if (pressbutton == "cancel") {
      submitform( pressbutton );
```

```
        return;
      }
      // verification of field content
      if (form.text.value == '') {
        alert( "Please enter something into the field." );
      } else {
        submitform( pressbutton );
      }
    }
    </script>
    <form action="index2.php" method="post" name="adminForm"
                                            id="adminForm"
     class="adminForm">
    <table border="0" cellpadding="3" cellspacing="0">
    <tr>
    <td>entry: </td>
    <td><input class="inputbox" type="text" size="50" maxlength="100"
                                                      name="text"
     value="<?php echo $row->text; ?>" /></td>
    </tr>
    </table>
    <input type="hidden" name="id" value="<?php echo $row->id; ?>" />
    <input type="hidden" name="option"
                                 value="<?php echo $option; ?>" />
    <input type="hidden" name="task" value="" />
    </form>
    <?php
    }
}?>
```

toolbar.mambobook.php

This file controls the various functions that can be invoked by clicking the icons in the toolbar and thereby represents the logic of the toolbar. The toolbar.mambobook.html. php file is merged with the presentation class.

Listing 7.8: toolbar.mambobook.php

```
<?php
defined( '_VALID_MOS' ) or ( 'Direct access to this file is
                                        prohibited.' );
require_once( $mainframe->getPath( 'toolbar_html' ) );
switch($task) {
  case "new":
  case "edit":
    menuMambobook::MENU_Edit();
    break;
  default:
    menuMambobook::MENU_Default();
    break;
}?>
```

toolbar.mambobook.html.php

Here the toolbar is assembled as shown in Listing 7.9. Procedures of the mosMenu class are called up twice: once for the list view and once for the edit view:

Figure 7.8: Toolbar in List mode

Figure 7.9: Toolbar in
Edit Mode

Listing 7.9: toolbar.mambobook.html.php

```php
<?php
defined( '_VALID_MOS' ) or ( 'Direct access of this file is
                                    prohibited.' );
class menuMambobook {
  function MENU_Default() {
    mosMenuBar::startTable();
    mosMenuBar::publishList();
    mosMenuBar::unpublishList();
    mosMenuBar::divider();
    mosMenuBar::addNew();
    mosMenuBar::editList();
    mosMenuBar::deleteList();
    mosMenuBar::spacer();
    mosMenuBar::endTable();
  }
  function MENU_Edit() {
    mosMenuBar::startTable();
    mosMenuBar::save();
    mosMenuBar::cancel();
    mosMenuBar::spacer();
    mosMenuBar::endTable();
  }
}?>
```

Test

After creating these files, you can administer the component from Mambo administration.

7.1.5 Create Installation Package

Besides the program files, you need two files with the installation text (see Listing 7.10) and the uninstallation text (see Listing 7.11). You also need an XML file as instruction file for the installer (see Listing 7.12).

install.mambobook.php

Listing 7.10: install.mambobook.php

```php
<?php
function com_install() {
  echo "Thank you for the installation. If you are having problems,
                                    contact hagen_39393@yahoo.de.";
}
?>
```

uninstall.mambobook.php

Listing 7.11: uninstall.mambobook.php

```
<?
function com_uninstall() {
echo "Thank you for using this component. The component will now be
                    uninstalled. If you have questions or comments,
                             please contact hagen_39393@yahoo.de.";
}
?>
```

mambobook.xml

Listing 7.12: mambobook.xml

```
<?xml version="1.0" ?>
<mosinstall type="component">
  <name>mambobook</name>
  <creationDate>03/29/2005</creationDate>
  <author>Hagen Graf</author>
  <copyright>GNU/GPL</copyright>
  <authorEmail>hagen_39393@yahoo.de</authorEmail>
  <authorUrl>www.alternative-unternehmensberatung.de</authorUrl>
  <version>1.0</version>
  <files>
    <filename>mambobook.php</filename>
    <filename>mambobook.html.php</filename>
  </files>
  <install>
    <queries>
      <query>DROP TABLE IF EXISTS `mos_mambo_book`;</query>
      <query> CREATE TABLE `mos_mambo_book` (
            `id` INT NOT NULL AUTO_INCREMENT,
            `text` TEXT NOT NULL,
            `published` TINYINT(1) NOT NULL,
            PRIMARY KEY (`id`) )
      </query>
    </queries>
  </install>
  <uninstall>
    <queries>
      <query>DROP TABLE IF EXISTS `mos_mambobook`;</query>
    </queries>
  </uninstall>
  <installfile>
    <filename>install.mambobook.php</filename>
  </installfile>
  <uninstallfile>
    <filename>uninstall.mambobook.php</filename>
  </uninstallfile>
  <administration>
    <menu>Mambobook</menu>
    <submenu>
      <menu act="all">edit entries</menu>
    </submenu>
    <files>
```

```
        <filename>admin.mambobook.php</filename>
        <filename>admin.mambobook.html.php</filename>
        <filename>mambobook.class.php</filename>
        <filename>toolbar.mambobook.php</filename>
        <filename>toolbar.mambobook.html.php</filename>
      </files>
    </administration>
</mosinstall>
```

To create the installation packet, you have to copy the created files into a directory and compress them all into a ZIP package named com_mambobook.zip. You can install this ZIP file with the installer component and if required, make it available for download.

Name	Size	Type	Date Modified
admin.mambobook.html.php	4 KB	PHP File	3/27/2005 7:31 PM
admin.mambobook.php	5 KB	PHP File	3/27/2005 8:19 PM
install.mambobook.php	1 KB	PHP File	3/27/2005 10:53 AM
mambobook.class.php	1 KB	PHP File	3/27/2005 8:19 PM
mambobook.html.php	1 KB	PHP File	3/27/2005 6:40 PM
mambobook.php	1 KB	PHP File	3/27/2005 6:40 PM
mambobook.xml	2 KB	XML Document	3/27/2005 8:34 PM
toolbar.mambobook.html.php	1 KB	PHP File	3/27/2005 8:19 PM
toolbar.mambobook.php	1 KB	PHP File	3/27/2005 8:19 PM
uninstall.mambobook.php	1 KB	PHP File	3/27/2005 8:18 PM
com_mambobuch.zip	7 KB	WinZip File	7/12/2005 7:51 AM

Figure 7.10: Files in the Mambobook Component

7.2 Modules

A module is lot simpler. You need two files; one for the logic (in this case, the presentation is handled mainly by the template) and an XML file for the installer module.

7.2.1 Source Code

mod_mambobook.php

Listing 7.13: mod_mambobook.php

```php
<?php
defined( '_VALID_MOS' ) or ( 'Direct Access to this location is not
allowed.' );
global $mosConfig_offset;
// SQL command to retrieve the last 5 entries from the DB
$database->setQuery("SELECT * FROM #__mambo_book LIMIT 5");
$rows = $database->loadObjectList();
echo "<ul>\n";
if ($rows) {
  // loop for the representation as list element <li></li>
  foreach ($rows as $row) {
    echo " <li>" . $row->text . "</li>\n";
```

```
    }
    echo "</ul>\n";
}
?>
```

mod_mambobook.xml

Listing 7.14: mod_mambobook.xml

```xml
<?xml version="1.0" encoding="iso-8859-1"?>
<mosinstall type="module" version="4.5.2">
  <name>Mambobook</name>
  <author>Hagen Graf</author>
  <creationDate>03/27/2005</creationDate>
  <license>GNU/GPL</license>
  <authorEmail>hagen_39393@yahoo.de</authorEmail>
  <authorUrl>www.alternative-unternehmensberatung.de</authorUrl>
  <version>1.0</version>
  <description><![CDATA[<p>With this module, 5 entries of the
       Mambobook test component are displayed .</p> <p> created
                by <a href = mailto:hagen_39393@yahoo.de >
           hagen_39393@yahoo.de </a></p><p>Have fun with this
                             module!</p><p><i><a href =
                "http://www.alternative-unternehmensberatung.de"
     target = "_blank" > alternativeunternehmensberatung.de </a>
                       </i></p><p>27/03/2005</p>]]></description>
  <files>
    <filename module="mod_mambobook">mod_mambobook.php</filename>
  </files>
</mosinstall>
```

7.2.2 Installation

Pack the two files in a ZIP package with the name mod_mambobook.zip and install it with the installer module:

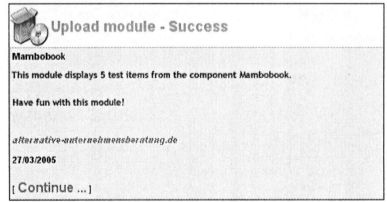

Figure 7.11: Installation Notice of the Mambobook Module

Activate the module in Site Module Manager.

7.2.3 View of the Website

You will see the entries on the website in the left module space:

Figure 7.12: Mambobook Module

7.3 Mambots

You need a Mambot to browse the list. Just like modules, create the PHP file with the logic (see Listing 7.15) and the XML file with the description (see Listing 7.16). Pack both files in a ZIP package, bot_mambobook.zip, and install it with the Mambot installer:

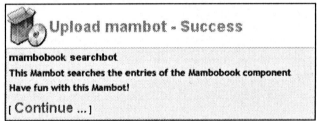

Figure 7.13: Installation Notice of the Mambobook Mambot

Listing 7.15: mambobook.searchbot,php

```php
<?php
defined('_VALID_MOS') or (Access not allowed');
$_MAMBOTS->registerFunction('onSearch','botSearchSections');
function botSearchSections($text, $phrase='', $ordering=''){
  global $database, $my;
  $stext = trim( $text );
  if ($text == '') {
    return array();
  }
  switch ( $ordering ) {
    case 'alpha':
      $order = 'text ASC';
      break;
    case 'category':
    case 'popular':
    case 'newest':
    case 'oldest':
    default:
      $order = 'text DESC';
  }
```

```
// search SQL string, that scans the field for substrings
// scaned
$query = "SELECT * FROM #__mambo_book"
    . "\n WHERE ( text LIKE '%$text%' )"
    . "\n AND published = '1'"
    . "\n ORDER BY $order";
$database->setQuery( $query );
$rows = $database->loadObjectList();
$count = count( $rows );
for ( $i = 0; $i < $count; $i++ ) {
  $rows[$i]->href = 'index.php?option=com_mambobookt&task=
                                  frei&id='. $rows[$i]-
    >secid .'&Itemid='. $rows[$i]->menuid;
  $rows[$i]->section = 'Mambobook List';
}
return $rows;
}
?>
```

Listing 7.16: mambobook.searchbot.xml

```xml
<?xml version="1.0" encoding="iso-8859-1"?>
<mosinstall version="4.5.2" type="mambot" group="search">
  <name>mambobook searchbot</name>
  <author>Hagen Graf</author>
  <creationDate>03/27/2005</creationDate>
  <license>GNU/GPL</license>
  <authorEmail>hagen_39393@yahoo.de</authorEmail>
  <authorUrl>www.alternative-unternehmensberatung.de</authorUrl>
  <version>4.5.2</version>
  <description>This Mambot searches the entries of the Mambobook
                                  component</description>
  <files>
    <filename mambot="mambobook.searchbot" > mambobook.searchbot.php
                                  </filename>
  </files>
  <params/>
</mosinstall>
```

If you activate the Mambot from the Mambots | Site Mambots menu, your list is searched via the search field on the website. After entering a search word, the field text in the database is scanned and the results are displayed in the common search mask as shown in Figure 7.14.

The searchbot is kept simple on purpose. The individual view of each list element should be linked to the place of discovery within the search results, so that the searcher can go there. Since we did not plan an individual view in our component, we cannot display a link here.

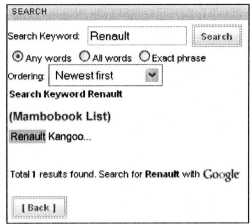

Figure 7.14: The Mambobook Searchbot in Action

7.4 End Remarks

This chapter gives an overview on producing components, modules, and Mambots.

You can use components from similar applications and develop them further. For example, our Mambobook component has one table view. Look for a component with an individual view (com_contact) and extend your Mambobook with this functionality. The same is true for specified parameters in modules. You can look for a model and create your own module.

What looks complicated at first sight is quite transparent on closer inspection.

Have fun experimenting!

Miscellaneous

A.1 Downloads

You can download the necessary software packages from their respective project pages or from the summary on our website at http://www.alternative-unternehmensberatung .de/component/option,com_weblinks/catid,2/Itemid,40/lang,en/. As the file packages offered on the website are suitable for a local installation, the examples in this book can be reconstructed accordingly. However, remember that several latest versions of the file packages are available on various other websites too.

A.1.1 Windows

The prerequisites for Windows are as follows:

- Development environment: xampplite (xampplite-win32-1.4.14.zip)
- Program package: Filzip (filzip.exe)

A.1.2 Linux

The prerequisites for Linux are as follows:

- Apache
- PHP
- MySQL environment

These are present and often preinstalled with the latest Linux distribution.

A.1.3 Operating System Independent

Section	File	Description
2.3	MamboV4.5.2-Stable.tar.gz	Mambo source code version 4.5.2
4.1.1	m4.5.2_germani.zip and m4.5.2_germanf.zip	Native language files (e.g. German)
5.1.2	com_simpleboard-1.0.4-beta2.zip	Forum components
5.1.3	german-SB1.0.4-beta2.zip	Native language file (e.g. German) for forum component
5.1.5	mod_simpleboard5.zip	Forum module
5.2.1	com_events-1.2.zip	Calendar component
5.2.4	mod_events_cal-1.1-beta.zip	Calendar module
5.2.5	bot_events_search-1.1.zip	Calendar Mambot
5.3.2	com_zoom_214_RC3.zip	Picture gallery component
5.3.3	zoom_media_gallery_2.1.4RC3.zip	Native language file (e.g. German) for picture gallery
5.4.1	com_akocomment20.zip	Comment component
5.4.1	cb_akocommentbot.zip	Comment component Mambot
5.5.1	MambelFish_1.5.zip	Mambelfish component
5.5.1	mbf_module.zip	Mambelfish module
5.5.4	mbf_searchbot.zip	Mambelfish search Mambot
6.2.6	mambobook.zip	Template
7.1.5	com_mambobook.zip	Component
7.2.2	mod_mambobook.zip	Module
7.3	bot_mambobook.zip	Mambot
Appendix A.3	MamboV4.5.2-API-Html.zip	Mambo API

Table A.1: Downloads

A.2 Templates

Templates contain many elements. The most important elements are the CSS arrays and the embedded PHP code.

A.2.1 CSS

In different Mambo versions, different names have become ingrained for certain arrays. These arrays are also called classes in CSS. I would like to show you four examples. If a class that does not exist in the CSS file is called, nothing changes in the display. Because of the multiplicity of versions and extensions, you are always well advised to look at the HTML code to get an overview of the classes used.

Head Area

Here you see the CSS definitions (Listing A.1) reflected in the head area and the respective areas on the website (Figure A.1). The CSS code is to serve as an example. Not all areas are provided with CSS examples. Look at the CSS files of predefined templates to find further examples:

Listing A.1: CSS Definitions: Head Area

```
.title {
  font-family: sans-serif;
  font-size: 20px;
  font-weight: bold;
  color: #000000;
  margin-left: 10px;
}
.button {
  font-family : Verdana, Arial, Helvetica, sans-serif;
  font-style : normal;
  font-size : 10px;
  font-weight : bold;
  background-color : #F0F0F0;
  color : #000000;
  border : 1px solid #CCCCCC;
}
```

Figure A.1: Head Area

Menu Area

Here you see the CSS definitions reflected in the menu area (Listing A.2) and in the respective areas of the website (Figure A.2):

Listing A.2: CSS Definitions: Menu Area

```
table.moduletable th {
   font-size : 11px;
   font-weight : bold;
   color : #000000;
   text-align : left;
   width : 100%;
   letter-spacing: 2px;
   text-indent: 5px;
   padding-bottom: 3px;
}
a.sublevel:link, a.sublevel:visited {
   padding-left: 1px;
   vertical-align: middle;
   font-size: 11px;
   color: #ff6600;
   text-align: left;
}
a.sublevel:hover {
   color: #ff9e31; text-decoration: none;
}
a.mainlevel:link, a.mainlevel:visited {
   display: block;
   color: #ffffff;
   font-weight: bold;
   background-image: url(../images/menu_bgr.png);
   background-repeat: no-repeat;
   width: 95%;
   text-indent: 15px;
   text-decoration: none;
   font-family: Verdana, Helvetica, Arial, sans-serif;
   line-height: 20px;
   margin-bottom: 1px;
}
a.mainlevel:hover {
   color: #333333;
}
.inputbox {
   font-family : Verdana, Arial, Helvetica, sans-serif;
   font-size : 10px;
   color : #000000;
   background-color : #F0F0F0;
   border : 1px solid #CCCCCC;
}
a:link, a:visited {
   color: #ff6600;
text-decoration: none;
}
a:hover {
   color: #ff3300;
   text-decoration: underline;
}
```

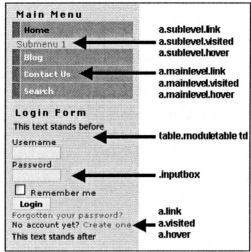

Figure A.2: Menu Area

Content Elements

Here you see the CSS definitions (Listing A.3) reflected in the content area and in the respective areas of the website (Figure A.3):

Listing A.3: CSS Definitions: Content Element

```css
.createdate {
  font-family : Arial, Helvetica, sans-serif;
  font-size : 10px;
  color : #999999;
  text-align : left;
}
.contentheading {
  font-family : Verdana, Arial, Helvetica, sans-serif;
  font-size : 12px;
  font-weight : bold;
  color : #ff9900;
  text-align : left;
}
.small {
  font-family : Verdana, Arial, Helvetica, sans-serif;
  font-size : 10px;
  color : #999999;
  text-decoration : none;
  font-weight : bold;
}
.contentpane {
  background : #dedede;
}
tr, td, p, div {
  font-family : Verdana, Arial, Helvetica, sans-serif;
  font-size : 11px;
  color : #333333;
}
```

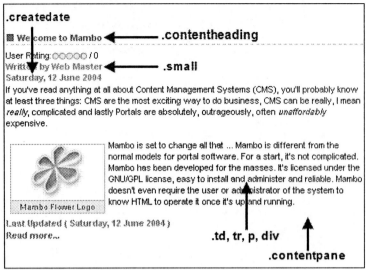

Figure A.3: Content Elements

News Overview

Here you see the CSS definitions (Listing A.4) reflected in the News overview and in the respective areas of the website (Figure A.4):

Listing A.4: CSS Definitions: News Overview

```
.sectiontableheader {
  background-color : #CCCCCC;
  color : #333333;
  font-weight : bold;
}
.sectiontableentry1 {
  background-color : #F0F0F0;
}
```

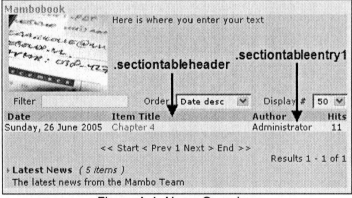

Figure A.4: News Overview

A.2.2 PHP and Other Modules in index.php

PHP code	Action
`<?php`	First line

`defined( '_VALID_MOS' ) or die`
`( 'Direct Access to this location,`
`is not allowed.' );`
`$iso = explode( '=', _ISO );`
`echo '<?xml version="1.0"`
`encoding="'.`
`$iso[1] .'"?' .'>';`
`?>`
`<!DOCTYPE html PUBLIC "-//W3C//DTD`
`XHTML 1.0 Transitional//EN"`
`"http://www.w3.org/TR/xhtml1`
`/DTD/xhtml1-transitional.dtd">`
`<html xmlns="http://www.w3.org/`
`1999/xhtml">`
	Here, direct access to the file is suppressed and the correct XHTML header is defined

HEAD	
`<?php mosShowHead(); ?>`	Creation of the metatags is defined as in Global Configuration

`if ( $my->id ) {`
`initEditor();`
`}`
	Initialization of the WYSIWYG editor

`<meta http-equiv="Content-Type"`
`content="text/html;`
`<?php echo _ISO; ?>" />`
	Specification of the correct content type

`<link href = "<?php echo`
`$mosConfig_live_site;`
`?>/templates/rhuk_solarflare_ii/css`
`/template_css.css"`
`rel="stylesheet" type="text/css"/>`
	Setting of the CSS file

BODY	
`<?php mosPathWay(); ?>`	The path of the page
`mosLoadModules ( '[ort]', [,` `$style])`	Loading of the module at the position of [ort]. If $style is given, its meaning is: 0 Module is displayed as a column in a table (`<td>...</td>`) 1 Module is displayed horizontally in a cell. -1 Module is displayed without surrounding table.

PHP code	Action
	-2 Module is displayed in the barrier-free xMambo format (<div>...</div>).
mosCountModules('[ort]')	Counting of the modules at position [ort]
<?php mosMainBody(); ?>	Content area
<?php include_once($GLOBALS['mosConfig_ absolute_path'] . '/includes/footer.php'); ?>	Footer

Table A.2: PHP Module in index.php

A.3 Mambo API

The **Application Programming Interface (API)** describes which functions are in the source code, at what place, and what they do:

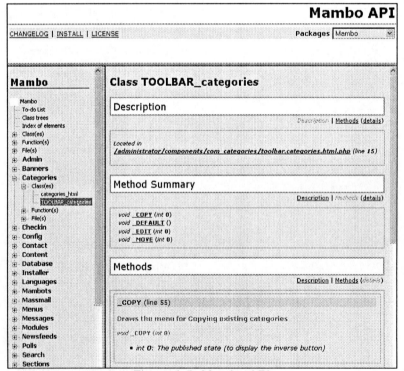

Figure A.5: Mambo API

It consists of static HTML pages, which are produced automatically by the source code. You can unpack the `MamboV4.5.2-API-Html.zip` file wherever you like and start it by double-clicking the `index.html` file. If you intend to develop your own components, the API is a good reference point.

A.4 Forgot your Admin Password?

If you have forgotten your admin password, you can change it directly in the database. To do that you need a tool like phpMyAdmin. In the xampplite environment, you can launch it in your browser using the URL `http://localhost/phpmyadmin`.

There you select the database you are using. There is a `mos_users` table in this database. In this table, look for the user admin. The password is encrypted using the MD5 algorithm (`http://en.wikipedia.org/wiki/MD5`). You can change it by selecting the MD5 entry in the option list, left of the field, and entering the password in plain text:

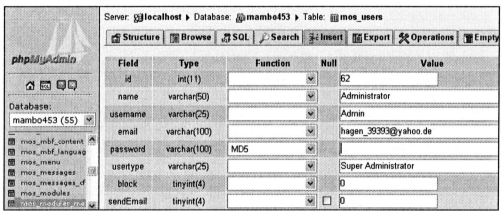

Figure A.6: Changing the Admin Password

Many providers also offer phpMyAdmin for the maintenance of your database.

Index

Thank you for buying Building Websites with Mambo: A Step by Step Tutorial

Packt Open Source Project Royalties

When we sell a book written on an Open Source project, we pay a royalty directly to that project. Therefore by purchasing *Buiding Websites with Mambo: A Step by Step Tutorial*, Packt will have given some of the money received to the Mambo project.

In the long term, we see ourselves and you—customers and readers of our books—as part of the Open Source ecosystem, providing sustainable revenue for the projects we publish on. Our aim at Packt is to establish publishing royalties as an essential part of the service and support a business model that sustains Open Source.

If you're working with an Open Source project that you would like us to publish on, and subsequently pay royalties to, please get in touch with us.

Writing for Packt

We welcome all inquiries from people who are interested in authoring. Book proposals should be sent to authors@packtpub.com. If your book idea is still at an early stage and you would like to discuss it first before writing a formal book proposal, contact us: one of our commissioning editors will get in touch with you.

We're not just looking for published authors; if you have strong technical skills but no writing experience, our experienced editors can help you develop a writing career, or simply get some additional reward for your expertise.

About Packt Publishing

Packt, pronounced 'packed,' published its first book "*Mastering phpMyAdmin for Effective MySQL Management*" in April 2004 and subsequently continued to specialize in publishing highly focused books on specific technologies and solutions.

Our books and publications share the experiences of your fellow IT professionals in adapting and customizing today's systems, applications, and frameworks. Our solution-based books give you the knowledge and power to customize the software and technologies you're using to get the job done. Packt books are more specific and less general than the IT books you have seen in the past. Our unique business model allows us to bring you more focused information, giving you more of what you need to know, and less of what you don't.

Packt is a modern, yet unique publishing company, which focuses on producing quality, cutting-edge books for communities of developers, administrators, and newbies alike. For more information, please visit our website: www.packtpub.com.

Learning eZ publish 3

Leaders of the eZ publish community guide you through this complex and powerful PHP-based content management system.

- Build content rich websites and applications using eZ publish
- Discover the secrets of the eZ publish templating system
- Develop the skills to create new eZ publish extensions

Building Websites with the ASP.NET Community Starter Kit

A comprehensive guide to understanding, implementing and extending the powerful and freely available application from Microsoft.

- Learn .NET architecture through building real-world examples
- Understand, implement, and extend the Community Starter Kit
- Learn to create and customize your own website
- For ASP.NET developers with a sound grasp of C#

Building Websites with OpenCms

A practical guide to understanding and working with this proven Java/JSP based content management system.

- Understand how OpenCms handles and publishes content to the Web
- Learn how to create your own complex, OpenCms website
- Develop the skills to implement, customize, and maintain an OpenCms website

SpamAssassin: A practical guide to Configuration, Customization, and Integration

An in-depth guide to implementing antispam solutions using SpamAssassin.

- Detect and prevent spam using SpamAssassin
- Install, configure, and customize SpamAssassin
- Integrate SpamAssassin with major mail agents and antispam services
- Use SpamAssassin to implement the best antispam solution for your network and your business requirement

Content Management with Plone

A comprehensive guide to the Plone content management system for Plone website administrators and developers.

- Design, build, and manage content rich websites using Plone
- Extend Plone's skins and content types
- Customize, secure and optimize Plone websites

Business Process Execution Language for Web Services

An architect and developer's guide to orchestrating web services using BPEL4WS.

- Specification of business processes in BPEL
- BPEL and its relation to other standards
- Advanced BPEL features such as compensation, concurrency, scopes, and correlations
- The Oracle BPEL Process Manager and BPEL Designer
- The Microsoft BizTalk Server 2004 as a BPEL server

Building Websites with Microsoft Content Management Server

A fast-paced and practical tutorial guide for C# developers starting out with MCMS 2002.

- Learn directly from recognized community experts
- Benefit from rapid developer level tutorials
- Develop a feature rich custom site incrementally
- Receive professional tips and tricks from developer newsgroups and online communities

Visit www.packtpub.com for information on all our books.

Printed in the United Kingdom
by Lightning Source UK Ltd.
106264UKS00002B/387-398